Basic Costing

For the 2003 Standards

April 2004

Workbook

GW00566239

In this April 2004 first edition

- Material designed for the new standards
- Layout designed to be easier on the eye – and easy to use
- Clear language and presentation

BPP
PROFESSIONAL EDUCATION

First edition April 2004

ISBN 0 7517 1938 2

British Library Cataloguing-in-Publication Data
A catalogue record for this book
is available from the British Library

Published by

BPP Professional Education
Aldine House, Aldine Place
London W12 8AW

www.bpp.com

Printed in Great Britain by W M Print
45-47 Frederick Street
Walsall, West Midlands
WS2 9NE

Contents

chapter 1

Making comparisons

Contents

1 Introduction

Management information helps managers plan, control and make decisions.

This chapter discusses how managers make comparisons between actual data and other data. In doing so they can assess the **significance** of the actual data for the period. Comparing current results with other data can make the information more useful. Comparisons may also help to show up any errors that have occurred.

2 Types of comparison

Many types of comparison are possible. The ones chosen depend on the needs of the individual and the organisation.

Common comparisons include the following.

2.1 Comparisons with previous periods

The most common comparison of a previous period is when **one year's final figures** are **compared** with the **previous year's**. A business's statutory financial accounts contain comparative figures for the previous year as well as the figures for the actual year. As financial accounts are sent to shareholders, this comparison is obviously of great interest to them.

Some companies' financial accounts contain figures for the last five years. Comparing the figures for five years may be more valuable than comparing the figures for two years. **Long-term trends** become more apparent over five years. If the comparison is only over two years, one or other year might be unusual for various reasons. This will distort the comparison.

For management accounting purposes year-on-year comparisons are insufficient by themselves. Management will wish to pick up problems a lot sooner than the end of the financial year. Hence comparisons are often made for management accounting purposes **month-by-month** or **quarter-by-quarter** (three months-by-three months).

2.2 Comparisons with corresponding periods

Making comparisons month-by-month or quarter-by-quarter is most useful when you expect figures to be reasonably even over time. However demand for many products fluctuates **season-by-season**.

Example: Seasonal fluctuations

A company making Christmas decorations had sales for the quarter ended 31 December that were considerably greater than sales for the previous quarter ended 30 September. For the quarter ended the following 31 March its sales decreased significantly again. Should its managers be concerned?

Based on the information given, we cannot tell. All the information tells us is that most people buy Christmas decorations in the three months leading up to Christmas. Comparing the December quarter's sales with the quarters either side is not very useful, because we are not comparing like with like. People are far more likely to buy Christmas decorations in the December quarter.

A far more meaningful comparison would therefore be to compare the December quarter's sales with those of the December quarter of the previous year, since the demand conditions would be similar.

This example demonstrates where comparisons with corresponding periods can be very useful, in businesses where the trade is **seasonal** (you would expect significant variations between adjacent periods).

2.3 Comparisons with forecasts

Businesses make forecasts for a number of purposes. A very common type of forecast is a **cash flow forecast.**

Example: Cash flow forecast

GEORGE LIMITED: CASH FLOW FORECAST FOR FIRST QUARTER

	Jan £	Feb £	Mar £
Estimated cash receipts			
From credit customers	14,000	16,500	17,000
From cash sales	3,000	4,000	4,500
Proceeds on disposal of fixed assets	-	2,200	-
Total cash receipts	17,000	22,700	21,500
Estimated cash payments			
To suppliers of goods	8,000	7,800	10,500
To employees (wages)	3,000	3,500	3,500
Purchase of fixed assets	-	12,500	-
Rent and rates	-	-	1,000
Other overheads	1,200	1,200	1,200
Repayment of loan	2,500	-	-
	14,700	25,000	16,200
Net surplus/(deficit) for month	2,300	2,300)	5,300
Opening cash balance	1,200	3,500	1,200
Closing cash balance	3,500	1,200	6,500

The purpose of making this forecast is for the business to be able to see how likely it is to have problems **maintaining** a **positive cash balance**. If the cash balance becomes negative, the business will have to obtain a loan or overdraft and have to pay interest costs.

At the end of the period management will **compare** the **actual figures** with the **forecast figures**, and try to assess why they differ. Differences are likely to be a sign that some of the **assumptions** made when drawing up the original forecast were **incorrect**. Hence management, when making forecasts for future periods, may wish to change the assumptions that are made.

2.4 Comparison with budgets

Most organisations divide their long-term goals into:

- **Objectives** (measurable steps towards achieving their goals)
- **Action plans** (detailed steps for achieving their objectives)

The action plans are often expressed in money and provide:

- An overall view for management
- Assurance that different departments' plans co-ordinate with each other

The financial plan is usually called a **budget**.

A **budget** is an organisation's plan for a forthcoming period, expressed in monetary terms.

You can use budgets to check that the plan is working by **comparing** the **planned results** for the day, week, month or year to date **with** the **actual results**.

Budgets, like forecasts, represent a view of the future. However the two are not identical. Forecasts represent a prediction of what is **likely to happen**, the most likely scenario. Budgets may be a **target** rather than a prediction. The target may be a very stiff one and it may be far more likely that the business fails to reach the target than that it does achieve the target. However management may feel that setting a stiff target may keep staff 'on their toes'.

Because comparison of actual data with budgeted data is a very important comparison for management purposes, we shall discuss this aspect in more detail later in this chapter.

2.5 Comparisons within organisations

Organisations may wish to compare the performance of departments and different sales regions.

Example: Analysis of results by sales area

PANDA LIMITED: ANALYSIS OF RESULTS BY SALES AREA

	Area 1 £'000	Area 2 £'000	Area 3 £'000	Total £'000
Sales (A)	600	500	150	1,250
Direct costs by areas:				
Cost of goods sold	320	250	60	630
Transport & outside warehousing	60	35	15	110
Regional office expenses	40	45	28	113
Salespeople's expenses	30	25	11	66
Other regional expenses	20	15	8	43
Total direct cost by areas (B)	470	370	122	962
Gross profit (A – B)	130	130	28	288

Alternatively comparisons may be on a product by product basis.

Example: Analysis of results by product

TEDDY LIMITED: ANALYSIS OF RESULTS BY PRODUCT

	Product A £'000	Product B £'000	Product C £'000	Total £'000
Sales	200	350	250	800
Variable costs of goods sold	95	175	90	360
Gross contribution	105	175	160	440
Variable marketing costs:				
Transport and warehousing	5	26	37	68
Office expenses	8	20	7	35
Sales salaries	15	44	25	84
Other expenses	2	7	6	15
Total variable marketing costs	30	97	75	202
Contribution	75	78	85	238

We shall discuss the importance of contribution in the next chapter.

2.6 Comparisons with other organisations

An obvious way of assessing how a business is performing in its chosen market is to **compare** its **results** and **financial position with** its **main competitors**. The main information that will generally be available about its competitors will be the competitor's annual statutory financial accounts. Thus the comparisons are generally made on an annual basis.

For management purposes comparisons with competitors' positions as shown in the accounts will often give only a broad indication of performance. The information available in statutory accounts is limited. For example the accounts will not give a product by product breakdown of sales, something which would be of great interest to management.

2.7 Comparisons with ledgers

Suppose you receive a query from a customer saying that you have sent him a statement saying that he owes £5,000, when he believes he only owes £1,000. You check the balance on his account in the sales ledger and indeed it is £5,000. However when you check the invoices that make up that balance, you see that two invoices totalling £4,000 were addressed to another customer, and have been wrongly posted in the sales ledger.

This example illustrates that you may need to compare the actual data on original documentation such as invoices with data in ledger accounts if **queries arise**.

2.8 Non-financial comparisons

As well as being made in **financial terms** (costs and revenues), you may make comparisons in other ways. For example you may compare units produced or sold. Other possible comparisons include measures of quality/customer satisfaction, time taken for various processes etc.

Example: A hospital casualty department

A hospital casualty department will aim to deal with incoming patients quickly, efficiently and effectively but numbers and types of patients are hard to predict. Comparing waiting times or cases dealt with per day will be misleading if one day includes the victims of a serious train crash and another covers only minor injuries. Long term comparisons might give a clearer picture and help to identify usage patterns (for example busy Saturday nights). Comparisons with other casualty departments might be even more revealing.

Activity 1.1

Do you think the comparisons given to the following individuals are the right ones to help them to assess the performance of their work teams?

(a)   Daily output in units compared with the same day, for the previous week, for a shift supervisor in a car factory

(b)   December sales value compared with the previous month for the sales manager of a firm trading in Christmas decorations

(c)   This year's examination results compared with last year for a secondary school headteacher

Helping hand. Think about the relevance and completeness of the information.

3 Identifying differences

Differences are only meaningful if they **compare like with like**.

For example if the heating bill for the summer quarter is less than that for the winter quarter, the difference does not tell you anything about organisational performance, only about the weather.

3.1 Changes in quantity

If production quantities change from the amount planned or the amount produced in previous periods, then obviously costs will change but by how much? The detailed techniques for dealing with this problem are beyond the scope of this Text. However in essence what you do is **adjust** the figures that you are comparing actual data with to take account of the changed quantities.

If production is 10% more than it was in the previous period, then we can expect the costs of direct materials to rise by about 10%. The effect on labour costs will depend on whether workers are paid a flat rate or by what they produce. Most factory overheads should not vary with the change in quantities produced.

Identifying differences only in financial terms may not be very helpful in finding out why they have actually occurred. For example if raw material expenditure is greater than forecast, this could be due to having spent a greater amount or used a greater quantity than planned. In this situation **reporting quantities as well as prices** will be helpful.

Activity 1.2

Here is part of a sales budget for an ice cream manufacturer.

MONTH	Jan	Feb	Mar	Apr	May	June	Jul	Aug
000 Gallons	1.0	1.0	1.1	1.1	1.2	1.4	1.4	1.5
Sales price £ per gall	8.00	8.00	8.00	8.00	8.00	8.50	8.50	8.50

(a) The sales department complains that they only get information on quantities sold and would like to know what revenue they have earned. They ask you to compare budgeted sales revenue with actual for the last three months (April, May and June). Where would you find the actual sales figures?

(b) You find the figures which are April £9,000, May £10,200 and June £11,800. The sales department telephones you to say that the price rise planned for 1 June was actually brought forward to 1 May.

Produce the report the sales department has asked for and compose a note to go with it, commenting on the effect of the price rise.

4 Reporting differences

The main point of reporting differences from the budget is to help managers to take the appropriate action. This makes it vital that they can **understand** the reports they get, ie that the reports are:

- **Relevant to their responsibilities**
- **Not cluttered up with unnecessary detail**

4.1 Reports

Here is a production cost report for week 32 for the department making cartons. Output was 5,000 units, as planned. Changes from week 31 have been calculated.

	Week 32 £	Week 31 £	Change £
Direct materials			
Cardboard	1,026	1,002	+24
Staples	498	499	-1
Glue	251	249	+2
Ink	99	100	-1
Total direct materials	1,874	1,850	+ 24
Direct labour	825	810	+15
Total direct costs	2,699	2,660	+39
Factory overheads	826	840	−14
TOTAL COST	3,525	3,500	+25

Some of these changes are very small and perhaps do not need to be shown in detail. An exception report could highlight the more significant changes on cardboard, direct labour and factory overheads.

Once you have identified important changes, you may need more detail to investigate them.

Activity 1.3

A ward sister in a private hospital has the following changes in ward costs reported as exceptional.

	Feb £	Mar £	Variance £
Nursing salaries	4,500	4,750	+250
Drugs and dressings	237	370	+133

(a)   Which of these costs do you think the sister can control?

(b)   She decides to investigate the drugs and dressings change and asks you to obtain information on budget, actual this year and actual last year. You obtain the following information from the management accounts and the budget preparation papers.

		Actual last year £	Actual this year £	Budget £
January	Drugs	175	182	180
	Dressings	62	72	70
February	Drugs	165	178	180
	Dressings	68	59	70
March	Drugs	170	300	180
	Dressings	60	70	70

Would you look any further and if so, why?

(c)   Do you think the drugs and dressings budget should be combined?

4.2 Comparison of non-financial information

Here is a report on the conveyancing department of a firm of solicitors for the year 20X1.

	Planned	Actual	Last year
Number of conveyances	300	290	295
Number of staff	3	3	2.5
£'000 Fees generated	155	156	145
£'000 Staff costs	62	65	56
£'000 Share of overheads	38	38	35
£'000 Departmental profit	55	53	54

This shows us that fees earned are well up on last year and better than planned, despite the fact that the number of conveyances are less than planned. Overheads are on target but staff costs are greater than expected.

Sometimes reports will include information in the form of **ratios or percentages** such as output per employee, profit as a percentage of revenue etc. In the example above, the number of conveyances per employee last year was 118, but this year it is only 96.7. Unless staff are doing more complex work, this needs investigation.

5 Comparing with budgets

5.1 Variances

We stated above that budgets can be used to check whether management's action plan is working. You compare the planned results for the day, week, month or year-to-date with actual results. Differences between actual figures and the budget are called **variances**.

Variance reporting is the reporting of differences between budgeted and actual performance.

Variances can be:

- **Favourable** if the business has more money as a result
- **Adverse** if the business has less money as a result

Favourable variances are not always good for the organisation. For example failure to recruit necessary staff will result in a favourable variance (less wages). It may, however, mean that business does not reach its production targets.

Reporting variances to the appropriate person draws attention to areas which are not running according to plan.

Activity 1.4

Here is an extract from a monthly cost report for a residential care home.

	Budgeted £	Actual £
Laundry	1,000	1,045
Heat and light	1,500	1,420
Catering	8,500	8,895
Nursing staff	7,000	6,400
Ancillary staff	10,600	10,950

(a) Calculate the variances for the above items in £ and % terms

$$\left(\text{Variance } \% = \frac{\text{Actual costs} - \text{Budgeted costs}}{\text{Budgeted costs}} \times 100\%\right)$$

(b) If company policy is to report only variances over £500, which would these be?

(c) If company policy is to report variances which are 5% or more of the budgeted amount, which would these be?

5.2 Budgets

Budgets are also used to allocate financial responsibility to individual managers. For example, the training manager will be responsible for expenditure on training. These responsible people are called **budget holders** and will have to decide what action to take if costs are higher or revenues lower than forecast. Reporting to them is sometimes called **responsibility accounting**.

The budget process will often document the key results required from budget holders in terms of **quantity** and **quality** as well as money. These targets will clarify how managers at different levels in the hierarchy can contribute to organisational objectives.

	Key objectives
Chief executive	Profit of £5,000
	2% growth in market share
	Improve employee relations
Production manager	No increase in cost per unit
	5% increase in units produced
	10% reduction in factory labour turnover
Factory supervisor	Reduce wastage of materials by 5%
	Reduce machine downtime by 10%
	Initiate monthly quality meetings

This information helps managers to perform their function of **controlling** the organisation. It is like a central heating thermostat with the budget as the temperature setting. Thermostats allow small variations around the setting but if the variation gets larger, they will take appropriate action (switch the boiler on or off) to control the temperature. In the same way, many organisations only report variances over a certain amount to avoid overwhelming managers with unnecessary detail.

5.2.1 Exception reporting

Exception reporting is the reporting only of those variances which exceed a certain amount or %.

You can classify variances as:

- **Controllable**: can be rectified by managers
- **Non-controllable:** are due to external factors beyond managers' control

Budget holders may be required to explain why either type of variance has occurred and should take whatever action is needed. If the variance is controllable, management can take action to rectify problems. If the variance is non-controllable, management may wish to revise their plan. Either way budget holders are not necessarily to **blame** for the variance.

Example: Comparison with budget

A manufacturer of copper pipes has budgeted for expenditure of £25,000 on copper in month 6 but actual expenditure is £28,000. Possible reasons for this include:

(a) **Price increase** by supplier. This may be controllable. The purchasing officer should try alternative suppliers.

(b) **World price rise** for copper. This is non-controllable. The budget may need revising for the rest of the year.

(c) **Higher factory rejection rate** of finished pipes. This is probably controllable but needs investigation. Is the raw material quality satisfactory? (if not, is this due to supplier, purchasing, warehousing?) Is the factory process at fault? (if so why? Poor supervision? Inadequate training? Machinery wearing out? - find out from the factory supervisors/managers).

You can see that reporting variances puts managers on the alert but only gives clues as to where the real problems lie.

Activity 1.5

A hospital decides to cut costs by reducing the number of cleaners employed by 10%. This results in a favourable variance in the budget reports. Is it good for the hospital?

Helping hand. Think of any other impacts a drop in a number of cleaners might have.

The ways in which managers use budgets is a part of a continuous process of planning, monitoring performance and taking action on variances. This is sometimes called the **control cycle** and can be illustrated as follows.

5.3 The control cycle

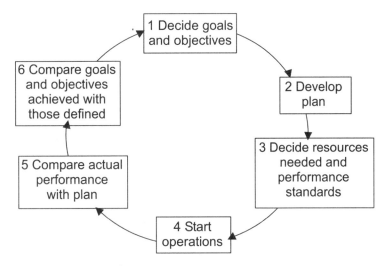

Activity 1.6

Here is an extract from a sales report for Region 3 in month 4 of the budget year (note that YTD stands for year to date, cumulative figures).

		£ actual	£ budgeted	£ actual YTD	£ budgeted YTD
Salesperson	Green	8,500	8,000	35,000	30,000
	Brown	7,600	8,000	25,000	30,000

(a)   What are the variances for each salesperson for month 4 and the YTD? Are they adverse or favourable?

(b)   Do you think they are controllable?

(c)   What action should the sales manager for Region 3 take?

Activity 1.7

A university librarian believes he exerts excellent management control because he has never overspent his budget and has tightened control over book stocks by reducing the loan period and increasing fines for overdue books. When applying for extra funds for a new book scanning system he is appalled to be told that library usage levels are far too low and that academic staff have resorted to keeping their own stocks of books and videos for loan to students. He suggests that these collections are immediately housed in the library, using staff from the information desk to catalogue and store them.

(a)   Are these suggestions sensible?

(b)   Is budget performance a good measure of library performance?

(c)   What other measures could you suggest?

5.4 Other uses of comparisons with budgets

Businesses obviously need to be **co-ordinated**. For example you cannot increase sales if you do not have the goods available, or increase stocks if you don't have the money to pay for them. Variance reporting is important in alerting management to unplanned changes in one area of the business which may affect another. For example an unplanned decrease in production will affect future sales unless it can be made up.

In some businesses, comparisons with budgets are used as a basis for extra **rewards** to managers such as bonuses, or profit sharing. This makes the accuracy of forecasting and reporting very important to managers. It may lead to arguments over which costs are controllable by individual budget holders or the way in which fixed overheads are **apportioned** between budget holders.

Don't forget that **other comparisons** are often used in addition to budget comparisons to assess performance more broadly.

5.5 Format of comparisons of budgeted data with actual data

Your organisation is likely to set a prescribed format. An example is shown below.

Example: Management accounts

CARING CROAT LTD: MANAGEMENT ACCOUNTS FOR JUNE

	Month (a) £'000	Budget (b) £'000	YTD (c) £'000	Budget for year Year (d) £'000	Plan (e) £'000
Sales	95	100	1,000	2,400	2,800
Cost of sales	48	45	460	1,000	1,000
Gross profit	47	55	540	1,400	1,800
Sales overheads	18	18	175	430	500
Administrative overheads	11	12	101	245	260
Net profit	18	25	264	725	1,040

Purposes of each column.

- **Month**. These are the actual figures for the month of June.

- **Budget**. The budgeted figures for the month may have been seasonally adjusted or they may be just the total figure for the year, divided by twelve.

- **Year to date**. These are the actual figures for the year up to the end of June.

- **Budget for year**. This is the budgeted figure for the year. It is adjusted for the actual figures to date, to provide a revised target for the year.

- **Year plan**. This is the original budget for the year.

Activity 1.8

The information below shows budgeted and actual sales for the first six months of the year in money and in units. The sales manager gets a half-yearly bonus if his sales efforts are successful.

	Month	1	2	3	4	5	6	Total YTD
Budget	Units 000	9.1	10.0	10.2	10.5	10.8	11.2	61.8
	£'000	18.2	20.0	20.4	21.0	21.6	22.4	123.6
Actual	Units 000	9.0	9.9	10.2	10.3	10.6	10.8	60.8
	£'000	18.0	19.8	21.4	21.6	22.3	22.7	125.8

(a) What other department(s) in the business will be directly affected by the results shown?

(b) Should the sales manager receive his bonus?

Activity 1.9

You are the Accounts Assistant at Mark Balding's clothes factory (Mark Balding's Ltd).

As part of your month-end procedures, you have produced the following performance report for production cost centres for April 20X1.

PERFORMANCE REPORT
PRODUCTION COST CENTRES
TOTAL COSTS - APRIL 20X1

	YEAR TO DATE 30.04.X1	
	Actual	*Budget*
	£	£
Materials	39,038	35,000
Labour	89,022	85,000
Expenses	18,781	15,000

Mark Balding is concerned that the year to date expenditure at the end of April 20X1 is not in line with expected expenditure and has asked you to report on any production cost variances which are more than 10% from budget.

Task

Produce a variance report with comments for Mark Balding.

Key learning points

☑ **Comparing actual results** with **other information** helps to put them in context and may show up errors.

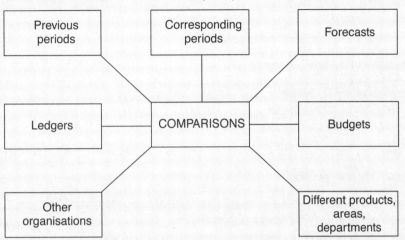

☑ Comparisons may be **financial** or **non-financial**.

☑ Choice of the comparison to make depends on the **characteristics** of the organisation, the **individual** and the **activity** being reported.

☑ When identifying differences you should ensure that you are **comparing like with like**.

☑ You should report differences in such a way that managers can **understand them** and pick out **vital information easily**. Comparisons should not be cluttered with irrelevant information or too much detail.

☑ Budget comparisons are popular because they show whether budget holders are **achieving** their **targets**.

☑ Variance reports help budget holders to perform their function of **control**. The reports are especially useful if they separate controllable from non-controllable variances.

☑ Variance reports can also alert the organisation to factors which may **harm** the planned **co-ordination** of activities.

☑ An organisation may use budget reports to determine **extra rewards** for successful managers.

☑ Budget reports may be **combined** with **other information** such as non-financial information, ratios etc.

Quick quiz

1   What is the difference between a budget and a forecast?

2   True or false?

    An adverse variance is one that is bad for the organisation.

3   Are these favourable or adverse variances?

    A   Increased advertising revenue
    B   Increased advertising expenditure
    C   Reduced distribution costs

4   What are the two possible reasons for a favourable variance on sales revenue in a manufacturing organisation?

5   Why is exception reporting popular?

    A   It avoids information overload and makes it possible to spot important differences
    B   It makes less work for the accounts department
    C   Because nobody is interested in small variances
    D   People don't want to waste their time reading long reports

6   The office manager is determined to keep to her budget. She has half the telephones disconnected and cancels all stationery orders. Is she doing a good job?

7   True or false?

    Managers sometimes argue about the way in which overheads are shared out, because this can affect their departmental profits and their bonuses.

Answers to quick quiz

1   A budget represents **targets** for the organisation, and so gives it something to strive for. A forecast is a realistic assessment of what is expected to happen.

2   True

3   A   Favourable
    B   Adverse
    C   Favourable

4   A higher level of sales or increased prices

5   A

6   No. Her job is to make sure the office functions smoothly.

7   True

chapter 2

Using management information for decision making

Contents

1 Introduction

Management information is used for lots of other purposes as well. You will cover some of these in your studies at Intermediate and Technician level, for example valuation of stock and assessment of risk.

This chapter provides an introduction to general **decision making**, to give you an idea of how management use the information that you provide.

We also discuss **pricing** which is one of the most important decisions management make. Set your prices too low, and you may not be able to cover costs. Set your prices too high and you may not be able to sell anything.

2 Making decisions

When providing management information for decision making, you must work out which costs and revenues are **relevant** to the decision. If in doubt, always clarify this with the person asking for the information.

2.1 Contribution

The manager of a factory making two products believes that one of them is much more profitable than the other and asks for a profit statement to compare them.

Profit statement

	Product A	Product B	Total
	£'000	£'000	£'000
Sale revenue	100	120	220
Less: Direct (variable) costs	(40)	(70)	(110)
Less: Fixed production overheads	(20)	(20)	(40)
Gross profit	40	30	70
Less: Other fixed expenses	(20)	(40)	(60)
Net profit/(loss)	20	(10)	10

Do you think the company should stop making product B?

The important idea here is that products can contribute towards fixed costs provided their:

Sales revenue is greater than variable costs.

So for example if 1,000 units of a product are sold at £40 per unit and the actual cost of making those units is £25 per unit, then the excess of revenue over costs = 1,000 (40 − 25) = £15,000. This £15,000 is available as a **contribution** to help pay for fixed costs such as insurance.

2.2 Marginal costing

The idea of products contributing towards fixed costs is very useful for many decisions. It is an important concept within a system of marginal costing.

Marginal costing is a system where only variable costs are charged as the cost of sale of an item. Fixed costs are charged to all products as an expense of the period.

In the example above a **marginal cost statement** would have made it clear that dropping Product B would decrease profits. The statement would look like this.

MARGINAL COST STATEMENT

	Product A	Product B	Total
	£'000	£'000	£'000
Sale revenue	100	120	220
Less: Variable costs	(40)	(70)	(110)
Contribution to fixed costs	60	50	110
Fixed production costs			(40)
Other fixed costs			(60)
Net profit			10

In the example, Product B is making a £50,000 contribution to the total fixed costs of £100,000.

Activity 2.1

(a) Calculate net profit if Product B is dropped and no other action is taken.
(b) What other options could be considered?

Activity 2.2

Axle Ltd makes canned dog food for supermarkets to sell as 'own brand'. Each can costs 30p in direct materials and labour and sells for 40p. Axle Ltd's fixed costs for next year are estimated at £50,000.

(a) How much does each can contribute towards fixed costs?

(b) How many cans will Axle have to sell next year to cover fixed costs?

(c) If forecast sales are 750,000 cans, what will budgeted profit be?

(d) If these sales leave some spare production capacity in the factory, should Axle accept a special order for 20,000 cans at 35p per can?

2.3 Breakeven

One way in which management use this information is to assess how safe the business is from making a loss.

Breakeven sales is the level of sales where:

Total contribution = Total fixed costs.

At this level the contribution from sales is just enough to cover fixed costs and the company makes neither a profit or a loss.

Margin of safety $= \dfrac{\text{Budgeted sales} - \text{Breakeven sales}}{\text{Budgeted sales}} \times 100\%$

Margin of safety $= \dfrac{\text{Actual sales} - \text{Breakeven sales}}{\text{Actual sales}} \times 100\%$

The calculation of the margin of safety provides a comparison between the sales needed to cover costs and the expected sales. In Activity 7.2 Axle Ltd's breakeven sales are where:

Total contribution = Fixed costs

Suppose X is the number of units sold needed to break even.

X (0.4 – 0.3) = 50,000
Therefore X = 500,000 units

As the margin of safety is a percentage, it can either be calculated using units sold or £ sales. Using units sold:

Margin of safety $= \dfrac{750,000 - 500,000}{750,000} \times 100\% = 33.3\%$

Put another way the safety volume of sales is 250,000 units. Axle Ltd will have to sell 250,000 less units before making a loss. The safety margin of 33.3% or 1/3 is quite large.

Activity 2.3

You are asked by the office manager to produce a report on the feasibility of your company installing a drinks vending machine in the office to sell coffee and tea at 30p per cup. At this price, she expects to sell 11,000 cups of tea and 17,000 cups of coffee. The information from the supplier tells you that you can purchase the machine for £2,600 or take a five year lease at £780 per year. An annual maintenance contract is available at £150 a year. The variable cost per cup is 22p for coffee and 20p for tea. Refer to chapter five for advice on report writing and produce a report which includes an assessment of whether income will cover costs, whether purchase or leasing is the best option and any other issues you think are important.

Helping hand. Remember to think about all the costs associated with the machine. What happens when the machine goes wrong?

3 Pricing

Pricing strategy depends upon two basic factors:

- **Cost**
- Market conditions

Obviously, in the long run the organisation must cover its costs or it will go out of business. Therefore the first step management must take when setting prices is to find out how much it costs to provide the goods or services. Management information systems should contain the necessary information.

Management must also take into account **market conditions.** The **degree** of **competition** in the market is an important influence. The demand for your product will probably decrease significantly if you increase its price, and make it more expensive than a similar product produced by your main competitor.

The **pattern of demand** must also be taken into account. As we have seen in previous chapters, the demand for some products varies significantly month-by-month. So for example warm clothing will be priced at full price during the winter. However it is likely to be sold off cheaply during the warmer weather of the spring and summer.

The **strategy** of the business setting the price is another important influence on pricing. For example, a firm trying to enter a new market with well-established competitors will probably have to undercut their price to gain customers from the competition. However a firm with very little competition will have less pressure to drive prices down. For instance the only plumber within a twenty-mile radius will be able to charge high prices.

More can generally be sold at a lower price than at a higher one. However firms may not necessarily make the biggest profits by reducing prices. Firms may find it more profitable to have lower sales at a higher price, and therefore higher profit per unit. This will depend on how sensitive **market demand** is to price changes.

Management information for pricing must therefore include **external information** about demand, competition, market price etc as well as internal cost information.

Activity 2.4

Bottleo Ltd makes a corkscrew which sells for £5. Budgeted sales this year are 20,000 units at a variable cost of £2.20 and fixed cost per unit of £1.80. Management want to increase profits and have asked the sales manager to research the likely effects of changes in selling price. His forecast is:

Selling price per unit £	Sales volume (units)
4.00	29,000
4.50	25,000
5.00	20,000
5.50	17,000
6.00	15,000

He has added a note that if an extra £6,000 is spent on advertising, all these sales forecasts can be increased by 10%.

What would you advise management to do?

Helping hand. Remember the importance of total contribution. How relevant are fixed costs?

Key learning points

☑ Management use management information to help them make a variety of business decisions.

☑ You will always need to know what information is relevant to the decision being made.

☑ **Marginal costing**, that is assessing the **contribution** which units sold make towards fixed cost, is one useful technique for assessing options for action.

☑ Pricing decisions depend on **information** about the **market** as well as **cost information**.

☑ Pricing decisions also depend on **company strategy**.

Quick quiz

1 If a firm reduces production, its............costs will go down but its............costs will remain the same.

2 Marginal costing charges only ....costs as the cost of sale of an item.

3 A business will break even when total .... equals fixed costs.

4 What is the margin of safety?

    A   The point below which the business goes bankrupt
    B   How much you need to sell to stay in business
    C   The difference between breakeven point and forecast or actual sales
    D   How far you will go below breakeven point if you raise prices

5 Pricing decisions require information on costs and ....

Answers to quick quiz

1 If a firm reduces production, its variable costs will go down but its fixed costs will remain the same.

2 Marginal costing charges only **variable** costs as the cost of sale of an item.

3 A business will break even when total contribution equals fixed costs.

4 C

5 Pricing decisions require information on costs and market conditions.

chapter 3

Cost information

Contents

1 Introduction

The aim of this chapter is to introduce you to some basic aspects of cost accounting.

- What are the objectives of a cost accounting system?
- What types of cost might be incurred in different kinds of organisation?

This chapter will provide you with the answers to questions such as these.

Later in this Interactive Text we will be returning to discuss in more detail many of the general principles and definitions that are introduced in this chapter. For now, you should try just to get a feel for what costing is all about, and the sort of terms that are used as the basic terminology of any cost accounting system.

2 What is cost accounting?

Where can an organisation's managers find the answers to the following questions?

- What was the cost of goods produced or services provided last month?
- What was the cost of operating a department last period?

Yes, you've guessed it, from the **cost accounting system.**

That was quite easy. But where can managers find the answers to these questions?

- What are the future costs of goods and services likely to be?
- How do actual costs compare with planned costs?

Well, you may be surprised, but the answer again is the **cost accounting system.**

In this Interactive Text you will be seeing how a cost accounting system also provides information to managers to help them **budget and plan for the future of the organisation.**

The managers of an organisation have the responsibility of planning and controlling the resources used. To do this effectively they need **sufficiently accurate** and **detailed** information, and the cost accounting system should provide this. **A cost accounting system analyses past, present and future data to provide the basis for managerial action.**

A wide variety of organisations uses cost accounting systems, ranging from manufacturing and service industries to government departments and charities. Therefore a cost accounting system might answer the following types of question.

- What is the cost of cleaning a hotel bedroom?
- What does it cost to provide street lighting to a particular area?
- What is the cost of taking an X-ray?
- What does it cost to provide a mobile library service?

This chapter provides a brief introduction to recording cost information.

3 Cost units and cost centres

Before we can go on to look at costs in detail, you need to understand a bit about the organisation of the cost accounting system.

3.1 Cost units

A **cost unit** is a unit of product which has a cost attached to it. The cost unit is the basic control unit for costing purposes.

A cost unit is not always a single item. It might be a batch of 1,000 if that is how the individual items are made. For example, a cost per 1,000 (or whatever) is often more meaningful information, especially if calculating a cost for a single item gives an amount that you cannot hold in your hand, like 0.003p. Examples of cost units are as follows.

- A batch of 1,000 pairs of shoes or 200 biros
- A passenger mile (for a bus company)
- A patient night (for a hospital)

Notice that the last two examples of cost units consisted of **two parts.** For instance a patient night is the cost of one patient staying for one night in a hospital. It would not be very meaningful to measure the 'cost per patient', because that would vary according to how long the patient stays. The 'cost per patient night', on the other hand, would not be affected by the length of stay of the individual patient.

3.2 Cost centres

Cost centres are the essential 'building blocks' of a costing system. They act as a collecting place for certain costs before they are analysed further.

There are a number of different types of cost centre, which include the following.

- A **department,** for example in a factory making cakes there could be a mixing department and a baking department.

- A **person,** for example the company solicitor may incur costs on books and stationery that are unique to his or her function.

- A **group of people,** for example the laboratory staff.

- An **item of equipment** such as a machine which incurs running and maintenance costs.

The number and types of cost centres that an organisation uses will depend on the organisation structure and on the type of product or service it produces.

Cost centres may vary in nature, but what they have in common is that they **incur costs**. It is therefore logical to **collect costs** initially under the headings of the various different cost centres that there may be in an organisation. Then, when we want to know how much our products or services cost, we simply find out how many cost units have passed through the cost centre and share out the costs incurred by that cost centre amongst the cost units.

25

4 The analysis of cost

4.1 Production costs

Let us suppose that you are holding a red biro. Look at your biro and consider what it consists of. There is probably a red plastic cap and a little red thing that fits into the end, and perhaps a yellow plastic sheath. There is an opaque plastic ink holder with red ink inside it. At the tip there is a gold plastic part holding a metal nib with a roller ball. How much do all these separate **materials** cost?

Now think about how the biro was manufactured. The manufacturer probably has machines to mould the plastic and do some of the assembly. How much does it cost, per batch of biros, to run the machines: to set them up so that they produce the right shape of moulded plastic? How much are the production line workers' wages per batch of biros?

Any of these separate production costs are known as **direct costs** because they can be traced directly to specific units of production.

4.2 Overheads

Overheads (or indirect costs) include costs that go into the making of the biro that you do not see when you dismantle it. You can touch the materials and you can appreciate that a combination of man and machine put them together. It is not so obvious that the manufacturer also has to do other things including the following.

- Lubricate machines and employ people to supervise the assembly staff
- Pay rent for the factory and for somewhere to keep the stock of materials
- Pay someone to buy materials, recruit labour and run the payroll
- Deliver the finished biros to the wholesaler
- Employ staff at head office to take orders and collect payments

Overheads are the biggest problem for cost accountants because it is not easy to tell by either looking at or measuring the product, what overheads went into getting it into the hands of the buyer. Overheads, or indirect costs, unlike direct costs, will not be identified with any single cost unit because they are **incurred for the benefit of all units rather than for any one specific unit.**

In this Interactive Text you will see how the cost accounting system tries to **apportion overheads (indirect costs) to each cost unit as fairly as possible.**

To summarise so far, the cost of an item can be divided into the following cost elements.

(a) Materials
(b) Labour
(c) Expenses

Each element can be split into two, as follows.

Materials	=	Direct materials	+	Indirect materials
+		+		+
Labour	=	Direct labour	+	Indirect labour
+		+		+
Expenses	=	Direct expenses	+	Indirect expenses
Total cost	=	Direct cost	+	Overhead

Total direct cost is sometimes referred to as **prime cost.**

Activity 3.1

List all of the different types of cost that a large supermarket might incur. Arrange them under headings of materials, labour and other expenses.

4.3 Fixed costs and variable costs

There is one other important way in which costs can be analysed and that is between fixed costs and variable costs.

(a) If you produce two identical biros you will use twice as many direct materials as you would if you only produced one biro. Direct materials are in this case a **variable cost**. They vary according to the volume of production.

(b) If you oil your machines after every 1,000 biros have been produced, the cost of oil is also a variable cost. It is an indirect material cost that varies according to the volume of production.

(c) If you rent the factory that houses your biro-making machines you will pay the same amount of rent per annum whether you produce one biro or 10,000 biros. Factory rental is an indirect expense and it is **fixed** no matter what the volume of activity is.

The examples in (b) and (c) are both indirect costs, or overheads, but (b) is a variable overhead and (c) is a fixed overhead. The example in (a) is a variable direct cost. Direct costs usually are variable although they do not have to be.

We are elaborating this point because it can be a source of great confusion. Variable cost is *not* just another name for a direct cost. The distinctions that can be made are as follows.

(a) **Costs are either direct or indirect, depending upon how easily they can be traced to a specific unit of production or service.**

(b) **Costs are either variable or fixed, depending upon whether they change when the volume of activity changes.**

Activity 3.2

Do you think the following are likely to be fixed or variable costs?

(a)   Charges for telephone calls made
(b)   Charges for rental of telephone
(c)   Annual salary of the chief accountant
(d)   Managing director's subscription to the Institute of Directors
(e)   Cost of materials used to pack 20 units of product X into a box

5 Product costing

5.1 Job costing

There are several different ways of arriving at a value for the different cost elements (material, labour and expenses) which make up a unit cost of production. The most straightforward case is where the thing to be costed is a **one-off item**. For example, a furniture maker may make a table, say, to a customer's specific requirements. From start to finish the table is a separately identifiable unit. The costs incurred to make that table are relatively easily identifiable. It will cost so much for the table top, so much for the legs, and so on. This form of costing is known as **job costing**.

5.2 Batch costing

An item like a biro, however, will be produced as one of a **batch** of identical items, because it would clearly be uneconomical to set up the machinery, employ labour and incur overheads to produce each biro individually. There might be a production run of, say, 5,000 biros. The cost of producing 5,000 biros would be calculated and if we wanted to know the cost of one biro we would divide this total by 5,000. The answer would however be a fraction of a penny and this is not very meaningful information.

This method of costing is called **batch costing** and it applies to many everyday items. So far as costing techniques are concerned, job and batch costing are very similar.

5.3 Unit costing

With batch costing and job costing, each cost unit is separately identifiable. The costs incurred could be traced to each table or to each batch of biros.

Some organisations may produce goods or services as a continuous stream of identical units, neither of which is separately identifiable for costing purposes. For example:

- A sauce manufacturer produces a continuous stream of identical bottles of sauce.
- A fast food restaurant serves a continuous supply of packets of chips with meals.

In these types of environment the costing system averages the costs incurred over all the units of output in a period.

$$\text{Cost per unit} = \frac{\text{total cost for period}}{\text{number of units of output in the period}}$$

Activity 3.3

Which method of costing (job, batch or unit costing) would be most appropriate for these businesses?

- A baker
- A transport company
- A plumber
- An accountancy firm
- A paint manufacturer

6 Functional costs

When we talk about functional costs we are not talking about a different **type** of cost to those we have met already, but about a way of grouping costs together according to what aspects of an organisation's operations (what **function**) causes them to be incurred.

A convenient set of functions is the following.

(a) **Production costs**. Materials and labour used and expenses incurred to make things and get them ready for sale.

(b) **Distribution and selling costs**. Costs incurred both to get the finished items to the point where people can buy them and to persuade people to buy them.

(c) **Administration costs**. These are the costs incurred in general office departments, such as accounting and personnel.

(d) **Financing costs**. The expenses incurred when a business has to borrow to purchase fixed assets, say, or simply to operate on a day to day basis.

These are not the only groupings of functional costs, nor are there rigid definitions of what is a production cost, what is an administration cost and so on.

7 Standard costs and variances

When we were talking about the questions to be answered by a cost accounting system we saw that the system might involve not only recording what costs were, but also predicting what they ought to be.

Recognising the usefulness of cost information as a tool for controlling what goes on, many businesses adopt what are known as **standard costs**.

- They decide what the unit cost of each element **should** be in advance of the actual cost being incurred.
- Once the cost has been incurred it is **compared** with the estimated standard cost.
- If there is a difference (a **variance**) somebody is asked to explain why.

To set a standard cost it is necessary not only to know what the level of cost was in the past but also to have an idea of what it is likely to be in the future. In Chapter 9 we shall look at the various problems involved in setting standard costs.

Standard costing is not an alternative to job, batch or unit costing. It is an approach that **can be used in addition** to those costing methods.

Activity 3.4

Explain the following terms in your own words.

(a)   Cost unit
(b)   Functional cost
(c)   Fixed cost
(d)   Standard cost
(e)   Indirect cost
(f)   Overhead
(g)   Cost centre
(h)   Variable cost
(i)   Direct cost

Key learning points

☑ Costs can be divided into three elements, **materials, labour** and **expenses.**

☑ A **cost unit** is a unit of product or service which has costs attached to it.

☑ A **cost centre** is something that incurs costs. It may be a place, a person, a group of people or an item of equipment.

☑ Costs can be analysed in different ways. For example direct, indirect, fixed, variable.

☑ Costs can also be analysed according to their function. For example production, distribution and selling, administration and financing costs.

☑ The most appropriate costing method for an organisation will depend on the nature of its products and services.

☑ Costing using standards is a good way of keeping a business under control.

Quick quiz

1 What is a cost unit?

2 Which cost elements make up overheads?

3 Name the three main types of costing method mentioned in this chapter.

4 List four types of functional cost.

Answers to quick quiz

1 A unit of product or service which incurs cost.

2 Indirect materials, indirect labour and indirect expenses.

3 Job costing, batch costing, unit costing

4
- Production costs
- Distribution and selling costs
- Administration costs
- Financing costs

chapter 4

Materials

Contents

1 Introduction

In the last chapter you learned about the various cost elements that go to make up the total cost of a product or service. In this chapter you will be going on to learn about the first cost element in detail: **materials.**

You will learn about how material stocks are **valued,** and how to maintain an effective **stock control system.**

2 Types of material

2.1 Raw materials

Raw materials are goods purchased for incorporation into products or services for sale.

Raw materials is a term which you are likely to come across often, both in your studies and your workplace. Examples of raw materials are as follows.

- Clay for making terracotta garden pots.
- Timber for making dining room tables.
- Paper for making books.

Activity 4.1

Without getting too technical, what are the main raw materials used in the manufacture of the following items?

(a)   A car
(b)   A box of breakfast cereal
(c)   A house (just the basic structure)
(d)   Your own organisation's products or services

Activity 4.2

How would you distinguish direct materials from indirect materials?

Activity 4.3

Classify the following as either direct or indirect materials.

(a)   The foil wrapping around Easter eggs
(b)   Paper used for the pages of a book
(c)   Lubricant used on sewing machines in a clothing factory
(d)   Plastic used to make audio cassette boxes
(e)   Shoe boxes

2.2 Work in progress

Work in progress is a term used to represent an intermediate stage between the manufacturer purchasing the materials that go to make up the finished product and the finished product. Work in progress is another name for **part-finished goods**.

Work in progress means that some work has been done on the materials purchased as part of the process of producing the finished product, but **the production process is not complete.** Examples of work in progress are as follows.

- Terracotta pots which have been shaped, but which have not yet been fired
- Tables which have been assembled, but which have not yet been polished

Work in progress must be subjected to further processing before it becomes **finished goods,** which are completed and ready for sale. Valuing work in progress is one of the most difficult tasks in cost accounting.

Activity 4.4

Distinguish between raw materials, work in progress and finished goods.

3 Buying materials

3.1 Purchasing procedures

All businesses have to buy materials of some sort, and this means that decisions have to be made and somebody has to be responsible for doing the **buying**. Large businesses have specialist **buying departments** managed by people who are very skilled at the job.

The following diagram shows the different purchasing procedures and the departments involved.

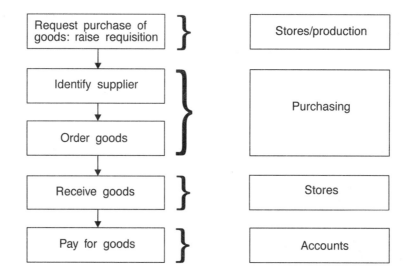

3.2 Purchasing documentation

We shall describe a manual system that might be used in a fairly large organisation. In reality it is likely that much of the procedure would be computerised, but this does not alter the basic principles or information flows.

3.2.1 Purchase requisition

The first stage will be that the department requiring the goods will complete a **purchase requisition** asking the **purchasing department** to carry out the necessary transaction. An example is shown below.

PURCHASE REQUISITION Req. No.			
Department _____ Suggested supplier:		Date Requested by: Latest date required:	
Quantity	Description and code no.	Estimated cost	
		Unit	£
Authorised signature:			

Note that the purchase requisition will usually need some form of **authorisation**, probably that of a senior person in the department requiring the goods **and** possibly also that of a senior person in the finance department if substantial expense is involved.

3.2.2 Order form

Once a **purchase requisition** is received in the purchasing department, the first task is to identify the most suitable **supplier**. Often the business will use a regular source of supply. The purchasing department may be aware of special offers or have details of new suppliers.

A **purchase order** is then completed by the purchasing department.

Purchase Order/Confirmation		Fenchurch Garden Centre Pickle Lane Westbridge Kent

Our Order Ref: Date

To

⌐(Address)⌐   Please deliver to the above address

                                               Ordered by:

                                               Passed and checked by:

                                               Total Order Value £

└   ┘

Quantity	Code No	Description	Unit cost £	Total £
		Subtotal		
		VAT (@ 17.5%)		
		Total		

Key

(a)   Sent to the supplier.
(b)   Legally binding document. Authorised personnel only should complete it.
(c)   Provides a means of checking that the goods received are the same as those ordered.
(d)   Copies sent to:

- The person who requisitioned the goods
- The stores department
- The accounts department

The **purchase order** is important because it provides a means by which the business can later **check that the goods received are the same as those ordered**.

3.2.3 Despatch note

Certain other documents may be completed before the goods are actually received. The supplier may acknowledge the order and perhaps indicate how long it is likely to take to be fulfilled. A **despatch note** may be sent to warn that the goods are on their way.

3.2.4 Delivery note

We now move to the stores department. When the goods are delivered, the goods inwards department will be presented with a **delivery note** or **advice note**. This is the supplier's document and a copy is signed by the person receiving the goods and this copy is returned to the supplier. If the actual goods cannot be inspected immediately, the delivery note should be signed **'subject to inspection'**.

3.2.5 Goods received note

Once the goods have been delivered they should be inspected and checked as soon as possible. A **goods received note (GRN)** will then be completed.

```
                                              ACCOUNTS  COPY

      GOODS  RECEIVED  NOTE  WAREHOUSE  COPY

  DATE: _ _7 March 20X1 _  TIME: _ _2.00 pm _ _ _ _     NO  5565

  ORDER NO: _ _ _ _ _ _ _ _ _ _ _ _ _ _ _ _ _ _ _ _.

  SUPPLIER'S  ADVICE  NOTE  NO: _ _ _ _ _ _ _ _ _ _ _ _.  WAREHOUSE A

  ┌────────────┬────────────┬──────────────────────────┐
  │ QUANTITY   │ CODE  NO   │ DESCRIPTION              │
  ├────────────┼────────────┼──────────────────────────┤
  │            │            │                          │
  │    20      │  TP 400    │ Terracotta pots, medium  │
  │            │            │                          │
  │            │            │                          │
  │            │            │                          │
  │            │            │                          │
  ├────────────┴────────────┴──────────────────────────┤
  │ RECEIVED  IN  GOOD  CONDITION:   L. W.    (INITIALS) │
  └─────────────────────────────────────────────────────┘
```

Key

(a)   Copy of **goods received note** sent to purchasing department so that it can be matched with the purchase order.

(b)   Copy of **goods received note** sent to accounts department so that it can be matched with the supplier's invoice.

The transaction ends with payment of the invoice (once any discrepancies have been sorted out).

Activity 4.5

Name four items that would be shown on a purchase order.

Helping hand. Thinking about the purpose of a purchase order will help you to reason through what details are required.

Activity 4.6

Draw a flow diagram illustrating the main documents involved in a materials purchase, from its initiation up until the time of delivery.

4 Valuing materials issues and stocks

When a stock item is issued from the stores to be used, say, in production, the cost accountant will record the **value of stock to be charged to the relevant cost centre.**

Example: Stock valuation

(a)   Suppose, for example, that you have 50 litres of a chemical in stock. You buy 2,000 litres to allow for the next batch of production. Both the opening stock and the newly-purchased stock cost £2 per litre.

	Litres	£
Opening stock	50	100
Purchases	2,000	4,000
	2,050	4,100

(b)   You actually use 1,600 litres, leaving you with 450 litres in stock. You know that each of the 1,600 litres used cost £2, as did each of the 450 litres remaining. There is no costing problem here.

(c)   Now suppose that in the following month you decide to buy another 1,300 litres, but have to pay £2.10 per litre because you lose a 10p discount if buying under 1,500 litres.

	Litres	Cost per litre £	Total cost £
Opening stock	450	2.00	900
Purchases	1,300	2.10	2,730
	1,750		3,630

(d)   For the next batch of production you use 1,600 litres, as before. What did the 1,600 litres used cost, and what value should you place on the 150 litres remaining in stock?

Solution

(a)   If we could identify which litres were used there would be no problem. Some would cost £2 per litre but most would cost £2.10. It may not, however, be possible to identify litres used. For instance, the chemical may not be perishable, and new purchases may simply be mixed in with older stock in a central tank. There would thus be no way of knowing to which delivery the 1,600 litres used belonged. Even if the chemical were stored in tins with date stamps it would be a tedious and expensive chore to keep track of precisely which tins were used when.

(b)   It may not therefore be possible or desirable to track the progress of each individual litre. However **we need to know the cost of the litres that we have used** so that we know how much to charge for the final product and so that we can compare this cost with the equivalent cost in earlier or future periods. We also **need to know the cost of closing stock** both because it will form part of the usage figure in the next period and for financial accounting purposes. Closing stock is often a significant figure in the financial statements and it appears in both the profit and loss account and the balance sheet.

(c) We therefore have to use a consistent method of pricing the litres which provides a reasonable approximation of the costs of the stock.

There are a number of different methods of valuing stock and the issues from stock.

- FIFO
- LIFO
- Weighted average cost

4.1 FIFO – First In First Out

This method values **issues at the prices of the oldest items in stock at the time the issues were made.** The remaining **stock will thus be valued at the price of the most recent purchases.** Say, for example ABC Ltd's stock consisted of four deliveries of raw material in the last month.

	Units		
1 September	1,000	at	£2.00
8 September	500	at	£2.50
15 September	500	at	£3.00
22 September	1,000	at	£3.50

If on 23 September 1,500 units were issued, 1,000 of these units would be priced at £2 (the cost of the 1,000 oldest units in stock), and 500 at £2.50 (the cost of the next oldest 500). 1,000 units of closing stock would be valued at £3.50 (the cost of the 1,000 most recent units received) and 500 units at £3.00 (the cost of the next most recent 500).

4.2 LIFO – Last In First Out

This method is the opposite of FIFO. **Issues will be valued at the prices of the most recent purchases**; hence **stock remaining will be valued at the cost of the oldest items.** In the example above it will be 1,000 units of **issues** which will be valued at £3.50, and the other 500 units issued will be valued at £3.00. 1,000 units of **closing stock** will be valued at £2.00, and 500 at £2.50.

4.3 Weighted average cost method

With this method we calculate an **average cost of all the units in stock whenever a new delivery is received.** Thus the individual price of the units issued *and* of the units in closing stock will be (22 September being the date of the last delivery) as follows.

$$\frac{\text{Total cost of units in stock at 22 September}}{\text{Units in stock at 22 September}}$$

The average price per unit will be $\frac{£8,250}{3,000} = £2.75$.

Example: FIFO, LIFO and Weighted average cost

Let's go back to the stock valuation example at the beginning of this section.

(a) **FIFO**

	Litres	Cost per litre £	Total cost £
Opening stock	450	2.00	900
Purchases	1,300	2.10	2,730
	1,750		3,630
Usage (oldest items first)	(450)	2.00	(900)
	1,300		2,730
Usage (1,600 – 450)	(1,150)	2.10	(2,415)
Closing stock	150		315

Total cost of usage is £900 + £2,415 = £3,315 and the value of closing stock is £315.

(b) **LIFO**

	Litres	Cost per litre £	Total cost £
Opening stock	450	2.00	900
Purchases	1,300	2.10	2,730
	1,750		3,630
Usage (most recent items first)	(1,300)	2.10	(2,730)
	450		900
Usage (1,600 – 1,300)	(300)	2.00	(600)
	150		300

Total cost of usage is £2,730 + £600 = £3,330 and the value of closing stock is £300.

(c) **Weighted average cost**

	Litres	Cost per litre £	Total cost £
Opening stock	450	2.000	900
Purchases	1,300	2.100	2,730
Stock at (£3,630/1,750)	1,750	2.074	3,630
Usage (at average price)	(1,600)	2.074	(3,318)
	150		312

Usage costs £3,318 under this method and closing stock is valued at £312.

For FIFO, LIFO and weighted average cost, note that the total of usage costs plus closing stock value is the same (£3,630) whichever method is used. In other words, **the total expenditure of £3,630 is simply split in different proportions between the usage cost for the period and the remaining stock value**. Note that there is no single correct method, each has its own advantages and disadvantages.

Activity 4.7

The following transactions took place during May. You are required to calculate the value of all issues and of closing stock using each of the following methods of valuation.

TRANSACTIONS DURING MAY

	Quantity Units	*Unit cost* £	*Total cost* £
Opening balance, 1 May	100	2.00	200
Receipts, 3 May	400	2.10	840
Issues, 4 May	200		
Receipts, 9 May	300	2.12	636
Issues, 11 May	400		
Receipts, 18 May	100	2.40	240
Issues, 20 May	100		
Closing balance, 31 May	200		
			1,916

Tasks

Calculate the value of all issues and of closing stock using each of the following methods of valuation.

(a)   FIFO
(b)   LIFO
(c)   Weighted average cost

4.4 Advantages and disadvantages of the FIFO method

Advantages	Disadvantages
It is a logical pricing method which probably represents what is physically happening: in practice the oldest stock is likely to be used first.	FIFO can be cumbersome to operate because of the need to identify each batch of material separately.
It is easy to understand and explain to managers.	Managers may find it difficult to compare costs and make decisions when they are charged with varying prices for the same materials.
The closing stock value can be near to a valuation based on the cost of replacing the stock.	

4.5 Advantages and disadvantages of the LIFO method

Advantages	Disadvantages
Stocks are issued at a price which is close to current market value. This is not the case with FIFO when there is a high rate of inflation.	The method can be cumbersome to operate because it sometimes results in several batches being only part-used in the stock records before another batch is received.
Managers are continually aware of recent costs when making decisions, because the costs being charged to their department or products will be close to current costs.	LIFO is often the opposite to what is physically happening and can therefore be difficult to explain to managers.
	As with FIFO, decision making can be difficult because of the variations in prices.

4.6 Advantages and disadvantages of weighted average cost method

Advantages	Disadvantages
Fluctuations in prices are smoothed out, making it easier to use the data for decision making.	The resulting issue price is rarely an actual price that has been paid, and can run to several decimal places.
It is easier to administer than FIFO and LIFO, because there is no need to identify each batch separately.	Prices tend to lag a little behind current market values when there is rapid inflation.

Activity 4.8

(a)   What is the main disadvantage of the FIFO method of stock valuation?
(b)   What is the main advantage of the LIFO method?
(c)   What is the main advantage and the main disadvantage of the weighted average cost method?

5 Stock control

Stock control is the regulation of stock levels, one aspect of which is putting a value to the amounts of stock issued and remaining. The stock control system can also be said to include ordering, purchasing and receiving goods and keeping track of them while they are in the warehouse.

The cost of purchasing stock is usually one of the largest costs faced by an organisation and, once obtained, stock has to be carefully controlled and checked.

5.1 Just-in-time

Some organisations operate a **just-in-time (JIT)** stock system. With a JIT system, supplies are ordered and delivered just as they are needed for production, and goods are manufactured just as they are needed for sales. **Stocks are therefore kept to a minimum,** and the system relies on **accurate forecasting** and **reliable suppliers.**

5.2 Buffer stock

Most organisations keep a certain amount of stock in reserve. This reserve of stock is known as **buffer stock.**

5.3 Reasons for holding stocks

- To ensure sufficient goods are available to meet expected demand
- To provide a buffer between processes
- To meet any future shortages
- To take advantage of bulk purchasing discounts
- To absorb seasonal fluctuations and any variations in usage and demand

5.4 Holding costs

If stocks are too high, **holding costs** will be incurred unnecessarily. Such costs occur for a number of reasons.

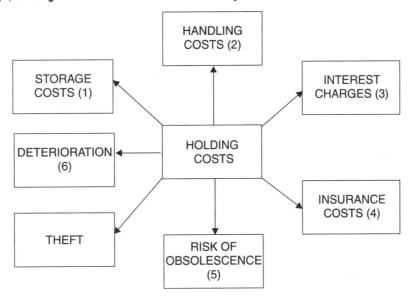

Key

(1) Higher stock levels require more storage space
(2) Higher stock levels require extra staff to handle them
(3) Holding stocks ties up capital on which interest must be paid
(4) The larger the value of stocks, the greater the insurance premiums

(5)   Stock may become out-of-date when held for long periods

(6)   Stock may deteriorate if stored for long periods

5.5 Ordering costs

If stocks are kept low, small quantities of stock will have to be ordered more frequently. This increases the amount of **ordering costs.** Ordering costs include the following.

- **Clerical and administrative costs** associated with purchasing, accounting for and receiving goods.
- **Transport costs**
- **Production run costs,** for stock which is manufactured internally rather than purchased from external sources.

5.6 Recording stock levels

One of the objectives of storekeeping is to **maintain accurate records of current stock levels.** This involves the recording of stock movements (issues from and receipts into stores). The most common system for recording stock movements is the use of **bin cards** and **stores record cards.**

5.6.1 Bin cards

A **bin card** shows the level of stock of an item at a particular stores location. It is kept with the actual stock and is updated by the storekeeper as stocks are received and issued. A typical bin card is shown below.

BIN CARD

Description .... Bin No: ....
                                          Code No: ....
Reorder Quantity .... Maximum: ....
                                          Minimum: ....
                                          Re-order Level: ....

Receipts			Issues			Balance	Remarks
Date	G.R.N No.	Quantity	Date	Req. No.	Quantity	Quantity	

Note that the bin card does not need to show any information about the cost of materials.

5.6.2 Stores record cards

Organisations will also maintain a **stores record card** for each stock item.

STORES RECORD CARD

Material: ....   Maximum Quantity: ....
Code: ....   Minimum Quantity: ....
                                              Re-order Level: ....
                                              Re-order Quantity: ....

Date	Receipts				Issues				Stock		
	G.R.N. No.	Quantity	Unit Price £	Amount £	Materials Req. No.	Quantity	Unit Price £	Amount £	Quantity	Unit Price £	Amount £

Details from **GRNs** and **materials requisition notes** (see later) are used to update **stores record cards**, which then provide a record of the **quantity** and **value** of each stock item in the stores. The stores record cards are normally kept in the cost department or in the stores office.

5.6.3 Stock control checks

The use of bin cards and stores record cards provides a **control check**. The balances on the bin cards in the stores can be compared with the balances on the stores record cards in the office.

5.6.4 Perpetual inventory system

The use of bin cards and stores record cards ensures that every issue and receipt of stock is recorded as it occurs so that there is a continuous clerical record of the balance of each item of stock. This is known as a **perpetual inventory system.**

5.7 Coding of materials

Each item held in stores must be **unambiguously identified** and this can best be done by numbering them with **stock codes**.

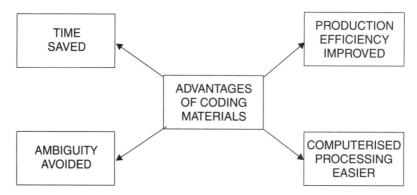

The digits in a code can stand for the type of stock, supplier, location and so forth. For example stock item A234/1279 might refer to the item of stock kept in row A, bay 2, bin 3, shelf 4. The item might be identified by the digits 12 and its supplier might be identified by the digits 79.

5.8 Issuing materials

Stocks are held so that they can be used to make products. Stocks are issued from stores to production in the first instance. This transaction will be initiated by the production department who will complete a **materials requisition note** and pass it to the warehouse.

5.8.1 Materials requisition note

MATERIALS REQUISITION NOTE

Material Required for: No.
  (Job or Overhead Account)
Department: Date:

Quantity	Description	Code No.	Weight	Price	Value £	Notes

Supervisor signature:

Key

(a)   The materials requisition note may also have a space for **the account code to be charged.**
(b)   If the material is for a **specific job**, the **job number** will be included on the materials requisition note.
(c)   The value of material issues will be based on either the FIFO, LIFO or weighted average cost method.

The stores department will locate the stock, withdraw the amount required and **update the bin card** as appropriate. The **stores record card** will also be updated.

Activity 4.9

An extract from the accounts code list of A Limited is as follows.

Cost centre codes		Expenditure codes	
Machining cost centre	100	Direct materials	100
Finishing cost centre	200	Indirect materials	200
Packing cost centre	300		
Maintenance cost centre	400		

Insert the correct account codes for the following materials issues from stores.

	Cost centre code no.	Expenditure code no.
Issue of packing materials to production	....	....
Issue of raw materials to machining centre	....	....
Issue of lubricating oils to maintenance	....	....
Issue of cleaning materials to finishing centre	....	....

Helping hand. The expenditure code will be 100, ie direct materials, if the materials are to become part of the finished product. If the materials cannot be traced directly to the finished product they should be coded as indirect materials.

5.8.2 Materials returned note

If the amount of materials required is overestimated the excess should be sent back to stores accompanied by a **materials returned note**. The form in our illustration is almost identical to a materials requisition note. In practice it would be wise to colour code the two documents (one white, one yellow, say) to prevent confusion.

MATERIALS RETURNED NOTE						
Material not needed for: (Job or Overhead Account) Department:					No. Date:	
Quantity	Description	Code No.	Weight	Price	Value £	Notes
Supervisor signature:						

5.8.3 Materials transfer note

There may be occasions when materials already issued but not required for one job can be used for another job in progress. In this case there is no point in returning the materials to the warehouse. Instead a **materials transfer note** can be raised indicating which job or cost centre is to be credited with the cost of material transferred, and which job or cost centre is to be debited. This prevents one job or cost centre being charged with too many materials and another with too little.

5.9 Stocktaking

Stocktaking involves **counting the physical stock on hand** at a certain date and then **checking this against the balance shown in the clerical records.** There are two methods of carrying out this process.

5.9.1 Periodic stocktaking

Periodic stocktaking is usually carried out annually and the objective is to count all items of stock on a specific date.

5.9.2 Continuous stocktaking

Continuous stocktaking involves counting and checking a number of stock items on a regular basis so that each item is checked **at least once a year**, and valuable items can be checked more frequently. This has a number of advantages over periodic stocktaking. It is less disruptive, less prone to error, and achieves greater control because discrepancies are identified earlier.

5.10 Stock discrepancies

There will be occasions when stock checks disclose **discrepancies between the physical amount of an item in stock and the amount shown in the stock records**. When this occurs, the cause of the discrepancy should be investigated, and appropriate action taken to ensure that it does not happen again.

5.10.1 Possible causes of discrepancies

- **Suppliers deliver a different quantity of goods than is shown on the goods received note (GRN).**
- **The quantity of stock issued to production is different from that shown on the materials requisition note.**
- **Excess stock is returned from production without documentation.**
- **Clerical errors may occur in the stock records.**
- **Breakages in stores may go unrecorded.**
- **Stock may be stolen.**

Activity 4.10

Give five reasons why stocktaking may identify discrepancies between the physical stock held and the balance shown on the stock records.

Key learning points

☑ **Raw materials** are goods purchased for incorporation into products or services for sale.

☑ **Work in progress** represents an intermediate stage between the manufacturer purchasing the materials that go to make up the finished product, and the finished product. It is another name for **part-finished goods**.

☑ A **finished good** is a product ready for sale or despatch.

☑ **FIFO** (First In First Out) prices materials issues at the prices of the oldest items in stock, and values closing stock at the value of the most recent purchases.

☑ **LIFO** (Last In First Out) prices materials issues at the prices of the most recent purchases, and values closing stock at the value of the oldest items.

☑ The **weighted average cost** method calculates an average cost of all stock items whenever a new delivery is received. The price for materials issues and for stock remaining after the issues will be the same.

☑ **Stock control** is the regulation of stock levels, which includes giving a value to the amounts of stock issued and remaining. Stock control also includes ordering, purchasing, receiving and storing goods.

☑ Materials held in stock are generally **coded** in order that each item is clearly identified.

☑ **Periodic stocktaking** is usually carried out annually, when all items of stock are counted on a specific date.

☑ **Continuous stocktaking** involves counting and checking a number of stock items on a regular basis so that each item is checked at least once a year.

Quick quiz

1 What are raw materials?

2 Items which are ready for sale or despatch are known as work in progress.

   ☐ True

   ☐ False

3 List the five documents which you are likely to use when buying materials.

   (a) ....

   (b) ....

   (c) ....

   (d) ....

   (e) ....

4 The goods received note is matched with two other documents in the buying process. What are they?

5   How would you calculate the cost of a unit of material using the weighted average cost method?

Weighted average cost $= \dfrac{A}{B}$

where   A = ……………………………

                               B = ……………………………

6   List three advantages of FIFO.

     (a)   ……………………………..

     (b)   ……………………………..

     (c)   ……………………………..

7   Which purchasing documents are used to update the stores record card?

8   What are the two methods of stocktaking that are commonly used?

Answers to quick quiz

1   Goods purchased for incorporation into products or services for sale.

2   ☑   False. Items which are ready for sale or despatch are known as finished goods.

3   (a)   Purchase requisition form
     (b)   Order form
     (c)   Despatch note
     (d)   Delivery note
     (e)   Goods received note (GRN)

4   The purchase order and the supplier's invoice.

5   A = Total cost of units in stock
     B = Number of units in stock

6   (a)   It is a logical pricing method
     (b)   It is easy to understand
     (c)   The closing stock can be near to a valuation based on the cost of replacing the stock

7   Goods received notes, materials requisition notes and materials returned notes.

8   Periodic stocktaking and continuous stocktaking.

chapter 5

Labour costs

Contents

1 Introduction

In this chapter you will be learning more about the second cost element we discussed in Chapter 3, labour.

You will be looking at a variety of aspects of **direct labour** and **indirect labour** and how labour costs are **identified, calculated, analysed and recorded**.

2 Determining labour costs

2.1 What are labour costs?

Labour costs include any or all of the following items.

- The gross amount of salary or wages paid to an employee
- Employer's National Insurance
- Amounts paid to recruit labour
- Amounts paid for staff welfare
- Training costs
- The costs of benefits such as company cars

The word labour is generally associated with strenuous physical effort but in the context of cost accounting it is not confined to manual work. **Labour costs** are the amounts paid to any employee, including supervisors, office staff and cleaning staff.

2.2 Determining labour costs

There are three ways in which labour costs can be determined.

- According to some prior agreement
- According to the amount of time worked
- According to the amount and/or quality of work done

Payment for most jobs is by a combination of the first two methods. There will be the following.

- A **basic wage** or **salary** which is agreed when the appointment is made.
- A **set number of hours** per week during which the employee is expected to be available for work.
- **Extra payments** for time worked over and above the set hours.
- **Deductions** for time when the employee is not available, beyond an agreed limit.

3 Recording labour costs

Records of labour costs fall into three categories.

- Records of agreed basic wages and salaries
- Records of time spent working

- Records of work done

In practice, timekeeping would probably be monitored by the production department or by the personnel department.

3.1 Attendance time

The bare minimum record of employees' time is a **simple attendance record** showing days absent because of holiday, sickness or other reason. Such a system is usually used when it is assumed that all of the employee's time is taken up doing one job and no further analysis is required.

The next step up is to have some **record of time of arrival, time of breaks and time of departure**. The simplest form is a **'signing-in' book** at the entrance to the building with, say, a page for each employee. Many employers use a **time recording clock** which stamps the time on a clock card inserted by the employee.

More modern systems involve the use of a plastic card like a credit card which is 'swiped' through a device which makes a **computer record** of the time of arrival and departure.

The next step is to analyse the hours spent at work according to what was done during those hours. Wages are calculated on the basis of the hours noted on the **attendance record.**

3.2 Detailed analysis of time: continuous production

Where **routine, repetitive work** is carried out it might not be practical to record the precise details. For example if a worker stands at a conveyor belt for seven hours the work can be measured by keeping a note of the number of units that pass through the employee's part of the process during that time. If a group of employees all contribute to the same process, the total units processed per period can be divided by the number of employees.

3.3 Detailed analysis of time: job costing

When the work is not of a repetitive nature the records required might be one or more of the following.

- Daily time sheets
- Weekly time sheets
- Job cards
- Route cards

3.3.1 Daily time sheets

These are filled in by the employee to indicate the **time spent on each job** (job code) or **area of work** (cost code).

Job No.	Start Time	Finish Time	Qty	Checker	Hrs	Rate	Extension

Time Sheet No. ....

Employee Name ....   Clock Code ....   Dept ....

Date ....   Week No. ....

3.3.2 Weekly time sheets

These are similar to daily time sheets but are passed to the cost office at the end of the week.

WEEKLY TIME SHEET

NAME _ _ _ _ _ _ _ _ _ _ _ _ _ _ _ _ _ _   Staff Number   WEEK end date D D M M Y Y

CLIENT or NON-CHARGEABLE TIME DESCRIPTION	HOURS WORKED Sat & Sun M T W T F	Total Hrs Incl O/T	O/T Hrs Incl	Client Number	Charge A/C Number	Hours to 2 Decimal Places
TOTAL					TOTAL	

Signed _ _ _ _ _ _ _ _ _ _ _ _ _ _ _   Authorised _ _ _ _ _ _ _ _ _ _ _ _ _ _   Date _ _ _ _ _ _ _ _

3.3.3 Job cards

Cards are prepared for each job (showing the work to be done and the expected time it should take) unlike time sheets which are made out for each employee. When an employee works on a job he or she records on the job card the time spent on that job.

```
                        JOB CARD

Department _ _ _ _ _ _ _ _ _ _ _ _ _ _      Job no _ _ _ _ _ _ _ _ _ _ _ _ _ _ _ _ _ _ _ _ _

Date _ _ _ _ _ _ _ _ _ _ _ _ _ _ _ _ _      Operation no _ _ _ _ _ _ _ _ _ _ _ _ _ _ _ _ _ _

Time allowance _ _ _ _ _ _ _ _ _ _ _ _      Time started _ _ _ _ _ _ _ _ _ _ _ _ _ _ _ _ _ _ _

                                            Time finished _ _ _ _ _ _ _ _ _ _ _ _ _ _ _ _ _ _

                                            Hours on job    _ _ _ _ _ _ _ _ _ _ _ _ _ _ _ _ _
```

Description of job	Hours	Rate	Cost

```
Employee no _ _ _ _ _ _ _ _ _ _ _ _ _ _ _      Certified by _ _ _ _ _ _ _ _ _ _ _ _ _ _ _ _ _ _

Signature _ _ _ _ _ _ _ _ _ _ _ _ _ _ _ _ _
```

3.3.4 Route cards

These are similar to job cards, except that they follow the job through the works and carry details of all operations to be carried out. They thus carry the cost of all operations involved in a job and are very useful for control purposes. **Production costs** are obtained from **time sheets/job cards/route cards.**

3.3.5 Salaried labour

You might think there is little point in salaried staff filling in a detailed timesheet about what they do every hour of the day, as their basic pay is a flat rate every month. In fact, in many organisations they are required to do so. There are a number of reasons for this.

- Such timesheets aid the creation of **management information** about product costs, and hence **profitability**.

- The timesheet information may have a direct impact on the **revenue the organisation receives.** For example a consultancy firm might charge their employees' time to clients. This means that if an employee spends an hour with a particular client, the client will be invoiced for one hour of the employee's time.

- Timesheets are used to record hours spent and so **support salaried staffs' claims for overtime payments**.

3.3.6 Idle time

There may be times when, through no fault of their own, employees cannot get on with their work. A machine may break down or there may simply be a temporary shortage of work. This is known as **idle time**

Idle time has a cost because employees will still be paid their basic wage or salary for these unproductive hours. Therefore there must be a record of idle time. This may simply comprise an entry on time sheets coded to 'idle time' generally. Alternatively a supervisor might enter the following details on separate **idle time record cards.**

- The time and duration of a stoppage
- The cause of the stoppage
- The employees made idle

Each stoppage should have a separate reference number which can be entered on time sheets or job cards as appropriate.

3.3.7 Payment by output

Piecework is a method of labour payment where workers are paid according to the amount of production completed.

The labour cost of work done by pieceworkers is determined from what is known as a **piecework ticket** or an **operation card**. The card records the total number of items (or **pieces**) produced and the number of rejects. Payment is only made for 'good' production.

OPERATION CARD				
Operator's Name	Total Batch Quantity			
Clock No	Start Time			
Pay week No .... Date	Stop Time			
Part No	Works Order No			
Operation	Special Instructions			
Quantity Produced	No Rejected	Good Production	Rate	£
Inspector	Operative			
Supervisor	Date			
PRODUCTION CANNOT BE CLAIMED WITHOUT A PROPERLY SIGNED CARD				

PROFESSIONAL EDUCATION

A **disadvantage of the piecework method** is that workers may be so concerned with the volume of output that they produce, that the **quality** of the goods might suffer.

Activity 5.1

(a)   Walter Wally is chief foreman in one of Sleepy Jeans Ltd's factories which is working on about thirty different jobs at any one time. He spends most of his day on his feet, dealing with personnel and technical problems as and when they arise.

How might Walter's time be analysed?

(b)   Peter Pratt is a cashier at Sleepy Jeans Ltd.

How might Peter's time be analysed?

3.4 Coding of job costs

In order to analyse labour costs effectively it is necessary to be able to link up different pieces of information in various ways. Organisations usually develop a series of codes for each of the following in order to make the analysis of labour costs more simple.

- **Employee number** (or team number)
- **Pay rate**, for example 'A' for £6 per hour, 'B' for £7 per hour
- **Department** and/or **location**
- **Job** or **batch number**
- **Client number**

Activity 5.2

Below are shown some extracts from the files of Sleepy Jeans Ltd.

Personnel files

	George	Paul	Ringo	John
Grade	A	B	C	D

Payroll - Master file

Grade	Basic rate per hour
A	£8.20
B	£7.40
C	£6.50
D	£5.30

Production report - labour

Job	Employee	Hours
249	George	14
249	Paul	49
250	George	2
250	John	107
250	Ringo	74

Task

You are required to calculate the labour cost of jobs 249 and 250.

4 Overtime, bonuses and absences

4.1 Overtime

One of the most common forms of **time work** is a **day-rate system**.

Wages (for a day-rate system) = Hours worked × rate of pay per hour

If an employee works for more hours than the basic daily requirement many organisations pay an extra amount, known as an **overtime payment.**

The overtime payment may simply be at the **basic rate**. If an employee earns £6 an hour he will be paid an extra £6 for every hour worked in addition to the basic hours.

Usually, however, overtime is paid at a **premium rate**. You will hear expressions like 'time and a third', ' time and a half' and so on. This means that the hourly rate for overtime hours is $(1 + \frac{1}{3})$ × basic rate or $(1 + \frac{1}{2})$ × basic rate.

Example: Overtime premium

Sleepy Jeans Ltd pays overtime at time and a quarter. Jo's basic hours are 9 am to 5 pm with an hour for lunch, but one particular Friday she worked until six o'clock. She is paid a basic wage of £6 per hour. How much did she earn on the Friday in question, and how much of this is overtime premium?

Solution

For costing purposes, the overtime premium must always be **identified separately** from the basic pay for the hours worked. Therefore the calculation is best presented as follows.

	£
Basic pay (8 × £6)	48.00
Overtime premium ($\frac{1}{4}$ × £6)	1.50
	49.50

4.1.1 Overtime premiums

The **overtime premium** in the example above is £1.50. This is an important point because overtime premium is usually treated as an **indirect cost**. This is quite reasonable if you think about it. If you and your colleague use identical calculators it is reasonable to suppose that they cost the same amount to produce. It might be that one was assembled at 10 o'clock in the morning and the other at 10 o'clock at night (ie during overtime hours), but this doesn't make the calculators different from each other. They should therefore have the same cost and so **most organisations treat overtime premium as an indirect cost or overhead** and do not allocate it to the products that happen to be manufactured outside basic hours.

There is one exception to this rule.

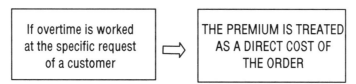

| If overtime is worked at the specific request of a customer | THE PREMIUM IS TREATED AS A DIRECT COST OF THE ORDER |

Activity 5.3

Peter works for Sleepy Jeans Ltd. Below is shown Peter's payslip for April. Peter spent the whole of April working on Job 472 without assistance. What is the direct labour cost of Job 472?

Employee: TORK, P Staff No: 017		Employer: SLEEPY JEANS LTD	
NI No: NA 123456C Tax Code: 344L Pay By: Cheque		Date: 30/4/X1 Tax Period: 1	
DESCRIPTION		AMOUNT	THIS YEAR
BASIC BONUS		1,327.42 145.83	
TOTAL PAY >>>		1,473.25	1,473.25
OTHER DEDUCTIONS INCOME TAX NATIONAL INSURANCE		282.41 93.44	282.41 93.44
NET PAY >>>		1,097.40	
OTHER ITEMS ADD EXPENSES REIMBURSED		301.28	
(HOL PAY ACCRUED 0.00) TOTAL NET PAY >>>		1,398.68	

Activity 5.4

Sleepy Jeans Ltd carries out a job for a customer that takes one employee, Dave, 50 hours in one week. The customer has asked that overtime is worked on the job in order that it may be completed as quickly as possible. Dave's basic hours are 9 am to 5 pm with an hour for lunch. He is paid a basic wage of £8 per hour and is paid overtime at time and a half. Two clerks in the accounts office are having a debate about how much of Dave's overtime premium should be charged to overheads. Jenny thinks it should be £60 and Mel says it should be £120.

Task

Try to resolve the dispute about the analysis of overtime premium.

4.2 Incentives and bonuses

Overtime premiums are paid to encourage staff to work longer hours than normal or to reward them for doing so. **Incentives and bonuses** are paid to encourage staff to work harder whatever the time of day.

Incentive schemes include the following.

- Piecework
- Time-saved bonus
- Group bonus scheme
- Profit-sharing scheme

4.2.1 Piecework

Pieceworking can be seen as an incentive scheme since the more output you produce the more you are paid. If you are paid 5p per unit produced and you want to earn £300 gross a week you know you have to produce 6,000 units that week (6,000 units × £0.05 = £300).

The system can be further refined by paying a different rate for different levels of production (**differential piecework**). For example the employer could pay 3p per unit for output of up to 3,500 a week, and 5p per unit for every unit over 3,500.

In practice, persons working on such schemes normally receive a **guaranteed minimum wage** because they may not be able to work due to problems outside their control.

Example: Piecework

An employee is paid £5 per piecework hour produced. In a 35 hour week he produces the following output.

	Piecework time allowed
	per unit
3 units of product A	2.5 hours
5 units of product B	8.0 hours

Task

Calculate the employee's pay for the week.

Solution

Piecework hours produced are calculated as follows.

Product A	3×2.5 hours	7.5 hours
Product B	5×8 hours	40.0 hours
Total piecework hours		47.5

Therefore employee's pay = $47.5 \times £5 = £237.50$ for the week.

Activity 5.5

Mr Shah works in one of Sleepy Jeans Ltd's factories. Using the information on piecework rates, complete the operation card shown below and calculate Mr Shah's gross wages for pay week number 17.

Number of units	*Piecework rates*
Up to 100 units a day	20p per unit on all units produced
101 to 120 units a day	30p per unit on all units produced
121 to 140 units a day	40p per unit on all units produced
Over 140 units a day	50p per unit on all units produced

OPERATION CARD

Operator's Name .... Shah, L ....   Total Batch Quantity .... - ....

Clock No ..... 7142 ....   Start Time ..... - ....

Pay week No ..... 17 .... Date W/E XX/XX/XX   Stop Time ...... - ....

Part No .... 713/V ....   Works Order No .... 14.AB ....

Operation ············· Drilling ....   Special Instructions ...... - ....

Quantity Produced	No Rejected	Good Production	Rate	£
Monday 173	14			
Tuesday 131	2			
Wednesday 92	-			
Thursday 120	7			
Friday 145	5			

Inspector .... ND ....   Operative .... LS ....

Supervisor .... AN ....   Date .... XX/XX/XX ....

PRODUCTION CANNOT BE CLAIMED WITHOUT A PROPERLY SIGNED CARD

4.2.2 Time-saved bonus

Suppose that a garage has calculated that it takes an average of 45 minutes for an engineer to perform an MOT test, but the job could be done competently in 30 minutes (ie the **standard time allowance** for an MOT is 30 minutes). It could encourage its engineers to do such work at the faster rate by paying **a bonus for every minute saved** on the job up to a maximum of 15 minutes.

The **standard time** allowed to produce a unit or complete a job is a measure of the **expected time** to produce a unit or complete a job.

Activity 5.6

Chris Steele works for Sleepy Jeans Ltd and is paid an hourly rate of £8 per hour. She is paid a bonus of 40% of any time saved against a standard allowance for work done. Last week she worked 35 hours and completed 90 units. The standard time allowed for one unit is 30 minutes.

Task

Calculate Chris's gross wages for last week.

4.2.3 Group bonus schemes

Sometimes it is not possible to measure individual effort because overall performance is not within any one person's control, for example a team of railway workers. In such cases, however, it is possible to measure **overall performance** of the team and **a bonus can therefore be paid to all those who contributed.**

Bonus payments are usually treated as indirect wages (or overhead).

4.2.4 Profit-sharing schemes

In a **profit-sharing scheme** employees receive **a certain proportion of their company's year-end profits.** The size of their bonus might also be related to the level of responsibility and length of service.

4.3 Absence from work

An employee may be absent from work for a variety of reasons, the most common are as follows.

- Holidays
- Sickness
- Maternity/paternity/adoption leave
- Training

The costs relating to absence through sickness, maternity/paternity/adoption and training are usually **treated as an overhead or indirect labour cost** rather than a direct cost of production.

Although some organisations treat holiday pay as an overhead, sometimes it is treated as a direct cost by charging an **inflated hourly rate.**

Time absent because of holidays is paid at the normal basic rate, as is absence on training courses as a rule. There are statutory minimum levels for maternity/paternity/adoption pay and sickness pay, but above these employers can be as generous (or otherwise) as they wish.

Activity 5.7

J Wain works for Sleepy Jeans Ltd and her latest time sheet and relevant information are shown below.

- J Wain is paid an hourly rate of £11 per hour.

- The first two digits of the code represent the cost centre to be charged.

  10   Finishing cost centre
  20   Packing cost centre
  30   Administration department
  40   Personnel department

- The last three digits of the code represent the expenditure code to be charged.

  100   Direct wages
  200   Indirect wages

- Administration, training and holiday time are classified as indirect time.

- Time spent on training courses is charged to the personnel department.

- Holiday pay is charged to the administration department.

Task

Use the information given to complete the time sheet and the accounts code boxes below.

WEEKLY TIME SHEET

Name J. Wain

Staff number 1 7 2 5 4

Week ending 0 9 1 2 0 1

	M	T	W	T	F	TOTAL Hours	£	CODE
Direct time								
Finishing	5	4		1	3			
Packing				6	3			
Direct total	5	4		7	6			
Administration								
Budget meeting	2				1			
Total admin	2				1			
Training and courses								
First Aid course		3						
Total training		3						
Holidays, sickness								
Holiday			7					
Total leave			7					
TOTAL	7	7	7	7	7	35		

Signed RS   Authorised LW

Key learning points

☑ **Labour costs** can be determined according to some prior agreement, the amount of time worked or the quantity/quality of work done.

☑ **Labour attendance time** is recorded on an **attendance record** or a **clockcard**. The analysis of time worked may be recorded on the following.

- Daily time sheets
- Weekly time sheets
- Job cards
- Route cards

☑ **Idle time** may occur when employees are not able to get on with their work through no fault of their own. Idle time has a cost and must therefore be recorded.

☑ **Piecework** is a method of labour payment where workers are paid according to the amount of production completed.

☑ The labour cost of work done by **pieceworkers** is recorded on a **piecework ticket/ operation card.**

☑ There are four main types of **incentive scheme**.

- Piecework
- Time-saved bonus
- Group bonus scheme
- Profit-sharing scheme

☑ If employees work more than their basic hours, many employers pay overtime. Usually, overtime is paid at a **premium rate.**

☑ **Overtime premium** is usually treated as an **indirect cost.** However, if overtime is worked at the specific request of a customer, the premium is a direct cost of the customer's job/order.

Quick quiz

1   What are the three basic ways of determining labour costs?

2   Which two documents can be used to record attendance time?

    (a)   ....

    (b)   ....

3   What is idle time? Give two examples of why it may occur.

4   What is overtime premium?

5   Tick the relevant box to indicate whether each of the following elements of labour cost would be treated as direct or indirect. All of the payments are made to, or on behalf of, **direct employees**.

	Direct labour cost	Indirect labour cost
(a) Overtime premium paid: (i) due to a temporary backlog in production		
(ii) at the specific request of a customer		
(b) Shift premium paid		
(c) Bonuses paid		
(d) Basic pay for overtime hours		
(e) Sick pay		
(f) Pay for diverted hours, spent cleaning machines		

6   List four types of incentive scheme.

7   Match the descriptions of remuneration schemes to the graphs below.

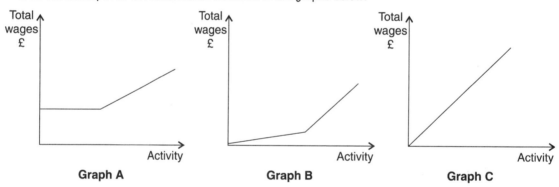

Graph A   Graph B   Graph C

Descriptions

(a)   A basic hourly rate is paid for hours worked, with an overtime premium payable for hours worked in excess of 35 per week.

(b)   A straight piece rate scheme is operated.

(c)   A straight piece rate scheme is operated, with a minimum guaranteed weekly wage.

BPP)))
PROFESSIONAL EDUCATION

Answers to quick quiz

1. Agreed basic wages and salaries, time spent, work done.

2 (a) Record of attendance
   (b) Clockcard

3 Time during which employees are being paid, but cannot get on with their work (though it is not their fault). It may occur when a machine breaks down or when there is a temporary shortage of work.

4 The extra amount paid, above the basic rate, for working overtime.

5

		Direct labour cost	Indirect labour cost
(a)	Overtime premium paid:		
	(i) due to a temporary backlog in production		✓
	(ii) at the specific request of a customer	✓	
(b)	Shift premium paid		✓
(c)	Bonuses paid		✓
(d)	Basic pay for overtime hours	✓	
(e)	Sick pay		✓
(f)	Pay for diverted hours, spent cleaning machines		✓

Explanations

(a) (i) **Indirect**. It would be 'unfair' to charge the items produced in overtime hours with the premium, just because they happen to be worked on during a direct employee's overtime hours.

     (ii) **Direct**. This overtime premium can be specifically identified with the customer's order.

(b) **Indirect**. This is usually treated as an indirect labour cost, again because it would be 'unfair' to charge the extra payment to items that happen to be produced during a shift where a premium is paid.

(c) **Indirect**. Unless the bonus payment can be traced to a specific cost unit, in which case it would be a direct cost of that unit.

(d) **Direct**. The basic pay for direct employees' overtime hours is a direct cost.

(e) **Indirect**. Direct employees' sick pay cannot be traced to a specific cost unit.

(f) **Indirect**. Diverted hours are those spent by direct employees doing indirect tasks, such as cleaning machines or counting stock.

6 (a) Piecework
   (b) Time-saved bonus
   (c) Group bonus scheme
   (d) Profit-sharing scheme

7 (a) Graph B
   (b) Graph C
   (c) Graph A

chapter 6

Expenses

Contents

1 Introduction

We have now looked at materials costs and labour costs in some detail in Chapters 4 and 5. Any other costs that might be incurred by an organisation are generally known as **expenses.** In this chapter we will be going on to look at a variety of **direct expenses** and **indirect expenses**.

2 Revenue and capital expenditure

2.1 Classification of expenses

Like materials and labour costs, expenses can also be divided into different categories. One such classification of expenses is as either **revenue expenditure** or as **capital expenditure.**

2.1.1 Capital expenditure

- **Capital expenditure** is expenditure which results in the acquisition of fixed assets.

- **Fixed assets** are assets which are acquired to provide benefits in more than one accounting period and are not intended to be resold in the normal course of trade.

Capital expenditure is not charged to the profit and loss account as an expense. Instead a **depreciation charge** is charged to the profit and loss account in order to write off the capital expenditure over a period of time. The depreciation charge is therefore an expense in the profit and loss account, so that the cost of the asset is spread over the years which benefit from its use.

Example: Depreciation charges

If an asset is bought for £20,000 and it is expected to last for 5 years and have no value at the end of that time, then for five years, £4,000 (£20,000 ÷ 5 years) will be charged as a **depreciation expense** to the profit and loss account.

2.1.2 Revenue expenditure

Revenue expenditure is expenditure which is incurred for one of the following reasons.

- For the purpose of the trade of the business, including administration expenses, selling and distribution expenses and finance charges.

- In order to maintain the existing earning capacity of fixed assets.

Revenue expenditure is charged to the profit and loss account in the period to which it relates.

2.2 Revenue and capital expenditure compared

Let us look at an example which should help you to distinguish between **revenue expenses** and **capital expenses.**

Example: Revenue items and capital items

Suppose that Bevan Ltd purchases a building for £30,000. A few years later it adds an extension to the building at a cost of £10,000. The building needs to have a few broken windows mended, its floors polished, and some missing roof tiles replaced. These cleaning and maintenance jobs cost £900.

Which items of expenditure are revenue expenditure and which are capital expenditure?

Solution

The original purchase cost (£30,000) and the cost of the extension (£10,000) are **capital expenditure** because they are incurred to acquire and then improve a fixed asset. The other costs of £900 are **revenue expenditure** because they are maintaining the existing earning capacity of the building.

The capital expenditure would be shared over several years' profit and loss accounts via a **depreciation expense.** The revenue expenditure would be charged as an **expense in the profit and loss account of the year it is incurred.**

2.3 Revenue and capital expenditure and costing

Revenue expenditure is of more relevance to the costing of products than capital expenditure. Capital expenditure is only of relevance when it is turned into revenue expenditure in the form of a **depreciation expense**.

2.4 Direct expenses and indirect expenses

A second major distinction that must be made is between **direct** and **indirect** expenses.

2.4.1 Direct expenses

Direct expenses are any expenses which are incurred on a specific product or service other than direct material cost and direct wages.

Direct expenses are charged to the product or service as part of the **prime cost** or **total direct cost**. Examples of direct expenses are as follows.

- The cost of **special** designs, drawings or layouts for a particular job
- The **hire of tools** or equipment for a particular job
- **Royalties** payable for each unit produced, for use of a copyright design

Direct expenses are also referred to as **chargeable expenses.**

2.4.2 Indirect expenses

Indirect expenses are expenses which cannot be identified in full with a specific item that is being costed. They are also known as overheads and are studied in detail in the next chapter.

Activity 6.1

The following information relates to Derbyshire Ltd.

State whether each of the following items should be classified as 'capital' or 'revenue' expenditure.

(a) Purchase of freehold premises

(b) Annual depreciation of freehold premises

(c) Solicitors' fees in connection with the purchase of freehold premises

(d) Costs of adding extra storage capacity to a mainframe computer used by the business

(e) Computer repairs and maintenance costs

(f) Cost of new machinery

(g) Customs duty charged on the machinery when imported into the country

(h) 'Carriage' costs of transporting the new machinery from the supplier's factory to the premises of the business purchasing the machinery

(i) Cost of installing the new machinery in the premises of the business

(j) Wages of the machine operators

3 Types of expense

Revenue expenditure other than materials and labour costs can arise for a number of different reasons.

BUILDINGS COSTS	⟶ Rent, Council tax, insurance
UTILITY COSTS	⟶ Gas, electricity, water rates, maintenance
STAFF COSTS	⟶ Health and safety, canteen, training
OPERATIONAL COSTS	⟶ Cleaning, maintenance, insurance, depreciation
FINANCE COSTS	⟶ Interest, bank charges
SELLING COSTS	⟶ Advertising, commission
PROFESSIONAL EXPENSES	⟶ Auditors' fees, solicitors' fees

PROFESSIONAL EDUCATION

4 Depreciation and obsolescence

4.1 Depreciation

We have already described depreciation as a method of writing off capital expenditure.

There are two principal methods of depreciating a fixed asset, the **straight line method** and the **reducing balance method**.

- The **straight line method** charges an equal amount of depreciation each period.

- The **reducing balance method** charges the largest amount of depreciation at the beginning of an asset's life. As the asset grows older the amount charged each period gets steadily smaller.

Example: Depreciation methods

Derbyshire Ltd purchased two fixed assets for £8,000 each. They will have no value after four years. One is depreciated over four years using the straight line method and the other is depreciated at the rate of 25% per annum on the reducing balance. What is the book value of each asset after four years and how much per year is charged to the profit and loss account as depreciation expense?

Solution

	Asset A		Asset B	
	Balance sheet	Profit and loss account	Balance sheet	Profit and loss account
	£	£	£	£
Capital cost	8,000		8,000	
Year 1 depreciation charge	(2,000)	2,000	(2,000)	2,000
c/f	6,000		6,000	
Year 2 depreciation charge	(2,000)	2,000	(1,500)	1,500
c/f	4,000		4,500	
Year 3 depreciation charge	(2,000)	2,000	(1,125)	1,125
c/f	2,000		3,375	
Year 4 depreciation charge	(2,000)	2,000	(844)	844
c/f	Nil		2,531	

The profit and loss account charge for asset A is calculated by dividing the £8,000 capital cost by four. For asset B it is calculated by taking 25% of the opening balance each year.

In order to decide which method is most appropriate we need to think a little more about why we are depreciating the asset at all.

4.2 The objectives of depreciation accounting

4.2.1 Objective 1

If an asset is purchased for £8,000 at the beginning of the year and sold for £6,000 at the end of the year then it is reasonable to conclude that the cost of owning the asset for a year is £2,000 (£8,000 – £6,000). This £2,000 is in addition to the costs of using the asset, like fuel and repairs costs.

If the business had not owned the asset it would not have been able to make its product or provide its service. It is therefore reasonable that the £2,000 cost should be recorded and charged as a cost of the product or service.

The first objective of depreciation accounting is therefore **to find some way of calculating this cost of ownership.**

4.2.2 Objective 2

Consider, however, the use of a machine that is constructed to do a specific job for a specific firm. It may last 20 years and yet be of no use to anybody else at any time in which case its resale value would be nil on the same day that it was bought. It is, however, hardly fair to charge the whole cost of the machine to the first product that it makes, or even to the first year's production. Very probably the products it is making in year 19 will be just as well made as the products made in year 1.

The second objective of depreciation accounting is therefore **to spread out the capital cost of the asset over as long a period as the asset is used.** In the example given there is a good case for spreading this cost in equal proportions over the whole 20 years.

4.2.3 Which method of depreciation accounting is best?

The answer to the question 'which method is best?' therefore depends upon the following.

- The asset in question
- The way it is used
- The length of time it is used
- The length of time it is useful in the light of changes in products, production methods and technology

4.3 Depreciation in practice

This sounds as if there are a lot of things to take into account, but in practice you may find that the method most often used is the **straight line method** because it is simple and gives a reasonable approximation.

Typical depreciation rates under the **straight line method** are as follows.

- Freehold land   Not depreciated
- Freehold buildings   2% per annum (50 years)
- Leasehold buildings   Over the period of the lease
- Plant and machinery   10% per annum (10 years)
- Motor vehicles   25% per annum (4 years)

Note that these are not rules. Businesses can choose whatever method or rate they think is most appropriate.

Sometimes you may encounter depreciation methods that try to measure the fall in value or the cost of use more accurately, for example, the **machine-hour method**.

Example: The machine-hour method

A machine costing £100,000 was purchased by Derbyshire Ltd in 20X3 and it is estimated that it will be sold for £5,000 at the end of its useful life. Experience has shown that such machines can run for approximately 10,000 hours before they wear out. What is the depreciation charge for the first year if the machine was used for 1,500 hours during the year?

Solution

The **machine-hour rate** is calculated as follows.

$$\textbf{Depreciation per machine hour} = \frac{\text{Cost} - \text{residual value}}{\text{Useful life}}$$

$$\frac{£(100,000-5,000)}{10,000 \text{ hours}} = £9.50 \text{ per machine hour}$$

The depreciation charge for the first year is therefore

1,500 hours × £9.50 = £14,250

4.4 Obsolescence

Obsolescence is the loss in value of an asset because it has been superseded, for example due to the development of a technically superior asset or changes in market conditions.

As the loss in value is due to quite another reason than the **wear and tear** associated with depreciation and because obsolescence may be rapid and difficult to forecast, it is not normal practice to make regular charges relating to obsolescence. Instead, **the loss resulting from the obsolescence should be charged as an expense direct to the costing profit and loss account when it arises.**

Activity 6.2

Derbyshire Ltd purchased a leather stamping machine last year. At the end of its first year of use the meter on the machine read 9728. It cost £4,000 and the suppliers are willing to buy it back for 20% of its cost at any time so that it can be used for parts. The sales literature claimed that it was capable of producing at least 100,000 stampings.

Task

What question will you need to ask the operational department concerned in order to determine whether the depreciation charge for the machine is a direct expense or an indirect expense?

Activity 6.3

Derbyshire Ltd purchased a machine three years ago for £75,000. Due to a change in government regulations, the component the machine produces can only be used for a further two years. At the end of two years, however, the machine can be sold for scrap for £5,000.

Task

Calculate the depreciation charge for the five years the machine is owned using both the straight line method and a rate of 42% per annum on the reducing balance.

5 Recording and coding expenses

In this chapter we are going to deal only with the initial stages of recording expenses. Much more detail will be found in the next chapter which explains how overhead costs are attributed to the total costs of individual units of product or service.

5.1 Direct expenses

Direct expenses (such as plant hire for a **specific** job or a solicitor's fees for drawing up a contract to provide a **specific** service) can simply be **coded to the appropriate job or client** when the invoice arrives. The expense would be recorded together with other direct costs against the relevant job or client numbers.

5.2 Indirect expenses

Indirect expenses **cannot be charged directly** to a **specific** cost unit. Instead a process of **allocation and apportionment** is necessary.

Allocation is the process by which whole cost items are charged direct to a cost unit or cost centre.

Indirect expenses are initially allocated where possible to the appropriate **cost centres**.

Cost centre type	Examples	
	Production	Service
Location	Finishing department	Hotel restaurant
Function	Sales department	Accounts department
Activity	Painting	Invoicing
Item of equipment	Spray-gun	Computer

The decision as to which cost centre is the appropriate one for an expense depends upon the type of expense. Some expenses will be **solely related to production** or to **administration** or to **selling and distribution** and can easily be **allocated** to the appropriate cost centre.

Other costs, however, will be shared between these various functions and so such costs cannot be allocated directly to one particular cost centre. Cost centres therefore have to be established for the **initial allocation** of such shared expenses. Examples of shared expenses include: rent, rates, heating and lighting, buildings maintenance and so on.

Example: Overhead allocation

The coding, analysis and recording of indirect expenses and other overheads at the initial stage may be demonstrated by the following example.

The weekly costs of Departments A and B include the following.

Wages of supervisor of Department A	£1,000
Wages of supervisor of Department B	£1,200
Indirect materials consumed in Department A	£400
Rent of premises shared by Departments A and B	£1,500

The cost accounting system includes the following cost centres.

Code	
101	Department A
102	Department B
201	Rent

Show the cost centres to which the costs will be initially coded.

Solution

(a)

	£	Code
Wages of supervisor of Department A	1,000	101
Wages of supervisor of Department B	1,200	102
Indirect materials consumed in Department A	400	101
Rent of premises shared by Departments A and B	1,500	201

(b) You may think that this is so obvious as not to be worth explaining. You will certainly not be surprised to be told that the next stage is to **share the rent paid between the two departments.** Why, you might ask, do we not split the cost of rent straightaway and not bother with cost centre 201?

(c) To answer this question consider the following extract from the cost accounts several months after the previous example. Cost centre 201 is no longer used because nobody could see the point of it.

	Cost centre	
	101	102
	£	£
Wages	1,172.36	1,415.00
Materials	73.92	169.75
Rent	638.25	1,086.75

You have just received a memo telling you that starting from this month (to which the above figures relate), Department A is to pay 25% of the total rent for the premises shared with Department B and Department B is to be split into two departments, with the new department (C) paying 37% of the remaining rent charge. The manager of Department B is standing over you asking you how much the department's new monthly rent charge will be.

(d) The answer is £815.06. More importantly the first thing you have to do to calculate the answer is to recreate the total cost information that used to be allocated to cost centre 201. This is not very difficult in the present example, but imagine that there were ten cost centres sharing premises and the cost information was recorded in a bulky ledger. Do you think it would have been easy to spot that the monthly rent had increased to £1,725?

5.3 Documentation

There are several ways in which this initial allocation could be documented. A common method is to put a stamp on the invoice itself with boxes to fill in, as appropriate. Suppose that Department C is given the code number 103. The rent invoice would be coded as follows.

%	Account codes no.	£	p
25.00	101	431	25
47.25	102	815	06
27.75	103	478	69
TOTAL	201	1725	00

Approved		Date	
Authorised		Date	
Posted		Date	

The dividing up of the total cost into portions to share it over the relevant cost centres is called **apportionment.** This process will be described in more detail in the next chapter.

5.4 Apportionment and responsibility accounting

The apportionment of costs raises another important question. It is unlikely that the managers of departments A, B and C have any **control** over the amount of rent that is paid for the building. They need to be **made aware that their part of the building is not free** but they are not **responsible** for the cost. The person responsible for controlling the amount of a cost such as this is more likely to be a separate manager, who looks after the interests of all of the company's buildings.

If cost centre 201 is maintained it can therefore be used to collect all the costs that are the **responsibility of the premises manager.** This approach is known as **responsibility accounting** and such cost centres can be called **responsibility centres**.

Activity 6.4

Derbyshire Ltd's accounts are prepared by Beancounters, a firm of accountants. Listed below are fifteen entries in the cash book of Beancounters. You are required to code the invoices according to the sort of expense you think has been incurred.

Nominal codes	Nominal account
0010	Advertising
0020	Bank charges
0030	Books and publications
0040	Cleaning
0050	Computer supplies
0060	Heat and light
0070	Motor expenses
0080	Motor vehicles
0090	Office equipment
0100	Printing, postage and stationery
0110	Rates
0120	Rent
0130	Repairs and maintenance
0140	Staff training
0150	Staff welfare
0160	Subscriptions
0170	Telephone
0180	Temporary staff
0190	Travel

Invoice received from	£	Code
Strange (Properties) Ltd	4,000.00	
Yorkshire Electricity plc	1,598.27	
Dudley Stationery Ltd	275.24	
Dora David (cleaner)	125.00	
BPP Publishing Ltd	358.00	
AAT	1,580.00	
British Telecom	1,431.89	
Kall Kwik (Stationers)	312.50	
Interest to 31.3.X3	2,649.33	
L & W Office Equipment	24.66	
Avis	153.72	
Federal Express	32.00	
Starriers Garage Ltd	79.80	

Activity 6.5

Beancounters is divided into three departments: audit, business services and tax. Which of the expenses listed in Activity 6.4 do you think are chargeable in total directly to individual clients, which are chargeable in total directly to departments and which cannot be split except by some method of apportionment?

Helping hand. There is no definitive answer to this activity, but take a few minutes to give it some thought. If you consider that you need more information, think about the queries that you would raise and who you would ask for the information.

Key learning points

☑ **Capital expenditure** is expenditure which results in the acquisition of fixed assets. Fixed assets are assets acquired to provide benefits in more than one accounting period. Capital expenditure is charged as an **expense** to the profit and loss account via a depreciation charge over a period of time.

☑ **Revenue expenditure** is expenditure which is incurred for the purpose of the trade of the business, or in order to maintain the existing earning capacity of fixed assets. It is charged as an **expense** to the profit and loss account in the period to which it relates.

☑ There are two principal methods of depreciating an asset, the **straight-line** method and the **reducing balance** method.

☑ **Obsolescence** is the loss in value of an asset because it has been superseded.

☑ **Direct expenses** are recorded by coding them to the appropriate job or client.

☑ **Indirect expenses** are initially **allocated** to appropriate cost centres and then spread out or **apportioned** to the cost centres that have benefited from the expense.

☑ In **responsibility accounting,** cost centres collect the costs that are the responsibility of the cost centre manager, and hence may be known as **responsibility centres.**

Quick quiz

1   Capital expenditure is charged to the profit and loss account at the end of an accounting period.

   [ ] True

   [ ] False

2   What is revenue expenditure?

3   The two main methods of depreciating an asset are:

   (a)   ....

   (b)   ....

4   When an asset loses value because it has been superseded due to the development of a technically superior asset, this is known as [   ]

5   The process by which whole cost items are charged direct to a cost unit or cost centre is known as:

   A   Expenditure
   B   Depreciation
   C   Allocation
   D   Obsolescence

6   What is responsibility accounting?

Answers to quick quiz

1   [✓] False

2   Revenue expenditure is expenditure incurred for the purpose of the trade of the business, or in order to maintain the existing earning capacity of fixed assets. It is charged as an expense in the period to which it relates.

3   (a)   Straight line method
     (b)   Reducing balance method

4   [Obsolescence]

5   C   Allocation is the process by which whole cost items are charged direct to a cost unit or cost centre.

6   When cost centre managers have responsibility for controlling the amount of the cost collected within certain cost centres, such cost centres are called responsibility centres.

chapter 7

Overheads and absorption costing

Contents

1 Introduction

Now that we have completed our detailed study of direct materials, direct labour and direct expenses, we can move on to look in more depth at **indirect costs,** or **overheads**. Overheads may be dealt with in a number of different ways. In this chapter we will be looking at **traditional absorption costing**.

2 What are overheads?

2.1 General overheads

An **overhead** is the cost incurred in the course of making a product, providing a service or running a department, but which cannot be traced directly and in full to the product, service or department.

Overheads are the total of the following.

- Indirect materials
- Indirect labour
- Indirect expenses

(Note that in the previous chapter we were looking at **expenses**, and whether they were direct or indirect.)

One common way of categorising overheads is as follows.

- Production overhead
- Administration overhead
- Selling overhead
- Distribution overhead

2.2 Production overhead

Production (or factory) overhead includes all indirect material costs, indirect wages and indirect expenses incurred in the factory.

- **Indirect materials** eg cleaning materials and maintenance materials
- **Indirect wages**, eg salaries of supervisors
- **Indirect expenses** eg rent of the factory and depreciation of machinery

2.3 Administration overhead

Administration overhead is all indirect material costs, wages and expenses incurred in the direction, control and administration of an organisation.

- **Depreciation** of office equipment
- **Office salaries**, including salaries of secretaries and accountants
- Rent, council tax, insurance, lighting, cleaning and heating of **general offices**

2.4 Selling overhead

Selling overhead is all indirect material costs, wages and expenses incurred in promoting sales and retaining customers.

- **Printing** and **stationery**, such as catalogues and price lists
- **Salaries** and **commission** of sales representatives and sales department staff
- **Advertising** and **sales promotion**, market research
- Rent and insurance of **sales offices**, bad debts and collection charges

2.5 Distribution overhead

Distribution overhead is all indirect material costs, wages and expenses incurred in making the packed product ready for despatch and delivering it to the customer.

- Cost of packing cases.
- Wages of packers, drivers and despatch clerks.
- Freight and insurance charges, depreciation of delivery vehicles.

3 What is absorption costing?

3.1 The objective of absorption costing

The objective of absorption costing is to include in the total cost of a product or service an appropriate share of the organisation's total overhead. By an appropriate share we mean an amount that reflects the amount of time and effort that has gone into producing the unit of product or service.

If an organisation had only one production department and produced identical units then the total overheads would be divided among the total units produced. Life is, of course, never that simple. **Absorption costing is a method of sharing overheads between a number of different products or services on a fair basis.**

3.2 Absorption costing procedures

The three steps involved in calculating the costs of overheads to be charged to cost units are

- **Allocation**
- **Apportionment**
- **Absorption**

Allocation is the process of assigning whole items of cost to cost centres. We studied the process of allocation in the previous chapter.

We shall now begin our study of absorption costing by looking at the first stage of **overhead apportionment.**

Activity 7.1

(a)   What is absorption costing?

(b)   What are the three stages of absorption costing?

4 Overhead apportionment – Stage 1

Apportionment is a procedure whereby indirect costs (overheads) are spread fairly between cost centres.

4.1 Sharing out common costs

Overhead apportionment follows on from overhead allocation. The first stage of overhead apportionment is to **identify all overhead costs** as production, administration, selling and distribution overhead. This means that the shared costs (such as rent and rates, heat and light and so on) initially allocated to a single cost centre must now be **shared out** between the other (functional) cost centres.

4.2 Bases of apportionment

It is important that overhead costs are shared out on a **fair basis** using appropriate bases of apportionment. The bases of apportionment for the most usual cases are given below.

Overhead	Basis of apportionment
Rent, council tax, heating and light, repairs and depreciation of buildings	Floor area occupied by each cost centre
Depreciation, insurance of equipment	Cost or book value of equipment
Personnel office, canteen, welfare, wages and cost office, first aid	Number of employees, or labour hours worked in each cost centre
Heating, lighting (see above)	Volume of space occupied by each cost centre

Don't forget that some overhead costs can be **allocated directly** to the user cost centre without having to be apportioned. For example indirect wages can be directly allocated because they relate solely to an individual cost centre.

Example: Bases of apportionment

Bravo Ltd incurred the following overhead costs.

	£
Depreciation of factory	1,000
Factory repairs and maintenance	600
Factory office costs (treat as production overhead)	1,500
Depreciation of equipment	800
Insurance of equipment	200
Heating	390
Lighting	100
Canteen	900
	5,490

Information relating to the production and service departments in the factory is as follows.

	Department			
	Production A	Production B	Service X	Service Y
Floor space (m²)	1,200	1,600	800	400
Volume (m³)	3,000	6,000	2,400	1,600
Number of employees	30	30	15	15
Book value of equipment	£30,000	£20,000	£10,000	£20,000

On what bases should the overhead costs be apportioned between the four departments? How much overhead would be apportioned to each department?

Solution

Item of cost	Basis of apportionment	Total cost	To Department			
			A	B	X	Y
		£	£	£	£	£
Factory depreciation	floor area	1,000	300	400	200	100
Factory repairs	floor area	600	180	240	120	60
Factory office	no. of employees	1,500	500	500	250	250
Equipment depn	book value	800	300	200	100	200
Equipment insurance	book value	200	75	50	25	50
Heating	volume	390	90	180	72	48
Lighting	floor area	100	30	40	20	10
Canteen	no. of employees	900	300	300	150	150
Total		5,490	1,775	1,910	937	868

Workings

Factory depreciation

Total floor space = (1,200 + 1,600 + 800 + 400)m²
= 4,000 m²

Factory depreciation is apportioned to the different departments as follows.

Production department A $= \dfrac{1,200}{4,000} \times £1,000 = £300$

Production department B $= \dfrac{1,600}{4,000} \times £1,000 = £400$

Service department X $= \dfrac{800}{4,000} \times £1,000 = £200$

Service department Y $= \dfrac{400}{4,000} \times £1,000 = £100$

The same method can be applied in order to calculate the apportionments of the other overheads.

Activity 7.2

Baldwin's Ltd is preparing its production overhead budgets. Cost centre expenses and related information have been budgeted as follows.

	Total £	Machine shop A £	Machine shop B £	Assembly £	Canteen £	Mainten-ance £
Indirect wages	78,560	8,586	9,190	15,674	29,650	15,460
Consumable materials (inc. maintenance)	16,900	6,400	8,700	1,200	600	-
Rent and rates	16,700					
Buildings insurance	2,400					
Power	8,600					
Heat and light	3,400					
Depreciation of machinery	40,200					
Value of machinery	402,000	201,000	179,000	22,000	-	-
Other information:						
Power usage – technical estimates (%)	100	55	40	3	-	2
Direct labour (hours)	35,000	8,000	6,200	20,800	-	-
Machine usage (hours)	25,200	7,200	18,000	-	-	-
Area (square metres)	45,000	10,000	12,000	15,000	6,000	2,000

Task

Calculate the overheads to be apportioned to the five cost centres.

5 Overhead apportionment – Stage 2

5.1 Reapportionment of service cost centre costs

The second stage of overhead apportionment concerns the treatment of service cost centres.

A factory is usually divided into **several production cost centres** and also **many service cost centres**. Service cost centres might include the **stores** or the **canteen**.

Only the production cost centres are directly involved in the manufacture of the units. In order to be able to **add production overheads to unit costs**, it is necessary to have all the overheads charged to the **production cost centres only**.

The next stage in absorption costing is therefore to **apportion the overheads of service cost centres to the production cost centres.** This is sometimes called **reapportionment.**

5.2 Methods of reapportionment

The reapportionment of service cost centre costs can be done by a number of methods. You only need to know about the following two methods.

- Direct method of reapportionment
- Step down method of reapportionment

Whichever method of reapportionment is used, **the basis of apportionment must be fair**. A different apportionment basis may be applied for each service cost centre. This is demonstrated in the following table.

Service cost centre	Possible basis of apportionment
Stores	Number or cost value of material requisitions
Maintenance	Hours of maintenance work done for each cost centre
Production planning	Direct labour hours worked in each production cost centre

5.3 Direct method of reapportionment

The **direct method of reapportionment** involves apportioning the costs of each service cost centre **to production cost centres only.**

This method is most easily explained by working through the following example.

Example: Direct method of reapportionment

Baldwin's Ltd incurred the following overhead costs.

	Production departments		Stores department	Maintenance department
	P	Q		
	£	£	£	£
Allocated costs	6,000	4,000	1,000	2,000
Apportioned costs	2,000	1,000	1,000	500
	8,000	5,000	2,000	2,500

Production department P requisitioned materials to the value of £12,000. Department Q requisitioned £8,000 of materials. The maintenance department provided 500 hours of work for department P and 750 hours for department Q.

Task

Calculate the total production overhead costs of Departments P and Q.

Solution

Service department	Basis of apportionment	Total cost	Dept P	Dept Q
		£	£	£
Stores	Value of requisitions (W1)	2,000	1,200	800
Maintenance	Maintenance hours (W2)	2,500	1,000	1,500
		4,500	2,200	2,300
Previously allocated and apportioned costs		13,000	8,000	5,000
Total overhead		17,500	10,200	7,300

Workings

(1) **Stores department overheads**

These are reapportioned as follows.

Total value of materials requisitioned $= £12,000 + £8,000$
$= £20,000$

Reapportioned to Department P $= \dfrac{£12,000}{£20,000} \times £2,000 = £1,200$

Reapportioned to Department Q $= \dfrac{£8,000}{£20,000} \times £2,000 = £800$

(2) **Maintenance department overheads**

These are reapportioned as follows.

Total hours worked $= 500 + 750 = 1,250$ hours

Reapportioned to Department P $= \dfrac{500}{1,250} \times £2,500 = £1,000$

$$\text{Reapportioned to Department Q} = \frac{750}{1,250} \times £2,500 = £1,500$$

The total overhead has now been shared, on a fair basis, between the two production departments.

Activity 7.3

The following information also relates to Baldwin's Ltd.

	Total £	Machine shop A £	Machine shop B £	Assembly £	Canteen £	Maintenance £
Indirect wages	78,560	8,586	9,190	15,674	29,650	15,460
Consumable materials	16,900	6,400	8,700	1,200	600	
Rent and rates	16,700	3,711	4,453	5,567	2,227	742
Insurance	2,400	533	640	800	320	107
Power	8,600	4,730	3,440	258		172
Heat and light	3,400	756	907	1,133	453	151
Depreciation	40,200	20,100	17,900	2,200	–	–
	166,760	44,816	45,230	26,832	33,250	16,632

Other information:

	Total	Machine shop A	Machine shop B	Assembly	Canteen	Maintenance
Power usage – technical estimates (%)	100	55	40	3	–	2
Direct labour (hours)	35,000	8,000	6,200	20,800	–	–
Machine usage (hours)	25,200	7,200	18,000	–	–	–
Area (square metres)	45,000	10,000	12,000	15,000	6,000	2,000

Task

Using the bases which you consider to be the most appropriate, calculate overhead totals for Baldwin's Ltd's three production departments, Machine Shop A, Machine Shop B and Assembly.

5.4 Step down method of reapportionment

This method works as follows.

Step 1 Reapportion one of the service cost centre's overheads to all of the other centres which make use of its services (production and service).

Step 2 Reapportion the overheads of the remaining service cost centre to the production departments only. The other service cost centre is ignored.

Example: Step down method of reapportionment

A company has two production departments and two service departments (stores and maintenance). The following information about activity in a recent costing period is available.

	Production departments		Stores department	Maintenance department
	1	2		
Overhead costs	£10,030	£8,970	£10,000	£8,000
Value of material requisitions	£30,000	£50,000	–	£20,000
Maintenance hours used	8,000	1,000	1,000	–

The stores and maintenance departments do work for each other as shown in the table below

	Production departments		Stores department	Maintenance department
	1	2		
Stores work done (100%)	30%	50%	–	20%
Maintenance work done (100%)	80%	10%	10%	–

Task

Using the information given above, apportion the service department overhead costs using the step down method of apportionment, **starting with the stores department**.

Solution

	Production departments		Stores department	Maintenance department
	1	2		
	£	£	£	£
Overhead costs	10,030	8,970	10,000	8,000
Apportion stores (30%/50%/20%)	3,000	5,000	(10,000)	2,000
Apportion maintenance				10,000
($^8/_9$/$^1/_9$)	8,889	1,111	–	(10,000)
	21,919	15,081	–	–

If the first apportionment had been the maintenance department, then the overheads of £8,000 would have been apportioned as follows.

	Production departments 1 £	2 £	Stores department £	Maintenance department £
Overhead costs	10,030	8,970	10,000	8,000
Apportion maintenance (80%/10%/10%)	6,400	800	800	(8,000)
			10,800	–
Apportion stores ($^3/_8$/$^5/_8$)	4,050	6,750	(10,800)	
	20,480	16,520	–	–

Note. Notice how the final results differ, depending upon whether the stores department or the maintenance department is apportioned first.

Activity 7.4

Elm Ltd has two service departments serving two production departments. Overhead costs apportioned to each department are as follows.

Production 1 £	Production 2 £	Service 1 £	Service 2 £
97,428	84,947	9,384	15,823

Service 1 department is expected to work a total of 40,000 hours for the other departments, divided as follows.

	Hours
Production 1	20,000
Production 2	15,000
Service 2	5,000

Service 2 department is expected to work a total of 12,000 hours for the other departments, divided as follows.

	Hours
Production 1	3,000
Production 2	8,000
Service 1	1,000

Task

The finance director has asked you to reapportion the costs of the two service departments using the direct method of apportionment.

Activity 7.5

When you show the finance director how you have reapportioned the costs of the two service departments, he says 'Did I say that we used the direct method? Well, I meant to say the step down method.'

Task

Prove to the finance director that you know how to use the step down method. (**Note.** Apportion the overheads of service department 1 first.)

6 Overhead absorption

6.1 Overhead absorption rate

Overhead absorption is the process whereby overhead costs allocated and apportioned to production cost centres are added to unit, job or batch costs. Overhead absorption is sometimes called **overhead recovery.**

Having allocated and apportioned all overheads, the next stage in the costing treatment of overheads is to add them to, or **absorb them into, cost units.**

Overheads are usually added to cost units using a **predetermined overhead absorption rate**, which is calculated using figures from the budget.

An overhead absorption rate for the forthcoming accounting period is calculated and used as follows.

Step 1   **Estimate the overhead** likely to be incurred during the coming period.

Step 2   **Estimate the activity level for the period.** This could be **total hours, units, or direct costs** or whatever measure of activity upon which the overhead absorption rates are to be based.

Step 3   **Divide the estimated overhead by the budgeted activity level.** This produces the predetermined overhead absorption rate.

Step 4   **Absorb** or **recover** the overhead into the cost unit by applying the calculated absorption rate.

Example: Overhead absorption rates

Channel Ltd makes two products, the Jersey and the Guernsey. Jerseys take 2 labour hours each to make and Guernseys take 5 labour hours.

Task

Calculate the overhead cost per unit for Jerseys and Guernseys respectively if overheads are absorbed on the basis of labour hours.

Solution

Step 1   Estimate the overhead likely to be incurred during the coming period

Channel Ltd estimates that the total overhead will be £50,000

Step 2   Estimate the activity level for the period

Channel Ltd estimates that a total of 100,000 direct labour hours will be worked

Step 3   Divide the estimated overhead by the budgeted activity level

$$\text{Overhead absorption rate} = \frac{\pounds50,000}{100,000\,\text{hrs}} = \pounds0.50 \text{ per direct labour hour}$$

Step 4   Absorb the overhead into the cost unit by applying the calculated absorption rate

	Jersey	*Guernsey*
Labour hours per unit	2	5
Absorption rate per labour hour	£0.50	£0.50
Overhead absorbed per unit	£1	£2.50

6.2 Possible bases of absorption

The most common absorption bases (or **'overhead recovery rates'**) are as follows.

- A rate per machine hour
- A rate per direct labour hour
- A percentage of direct labour cost
- A percentage of direct materials cost
- A percentage of total direct cost (prime cost)
- A rate per unit
- A percentage of factory cost (for administration overhead)
- A percentage of sales value or factory cost (for selling and distribution overhead)

The most appropriate basis for production overhead depends largely on the organisation concerned. As with apportionment it is a matter of being fair.

Many factories tend to use the **direct labour hour rate** or **machine hour rate** in preference to a rate based on a percentage of direct materials cost, wages or prime cost.

A **machine hour rate** would be used in departments where production is controlled or dictated by machines. A **direct labour hour basis** is more appropriate in a labour intensive environment.

Example: Bases of absorption

The budgeted production overheads and other budget data of Bases Ltd are as follows.

Budget	Production dept X	Production dept Y
Production overhead cost	£36,000	£5,000
Direct materials cost	£32,000	
Direct labour cost	£40,000	
Machine hours	10,000	
Direct labour hours	18,000	
Units of production		1,000

What would the absorption rate be for each department using the various bases of apportionment?

Solution

(a) **Department X**

(i) Rate per machine hour $\dfrac{£36,000}{10,000 \text{ hrs}}$ = £3.60 per machine hour

(ii) Rate per direct labour hour $\dfrac{£36,000}{18,000 \text{ hrs}}$ = £2 per direct labour hour

(iii) % of direct labour cost $\dfrac{£36,000}{£40,000} \times 100\%$ = 90%

(iv) % of direct materials cost $\dfrac{£36,000}{£32,000} \times 100\%$ = 112.5%

(v) % of total direct cost $\dfrac{£36,000}{£72,000} \times 100\%$ = 50%

(b) For **department Y** the absorption rate will be based on units of output.

$\dfrac{£5,000}{1,000 \text{ units}}$ = £5 per unit produced

Activity 7.6

(a) If production overheads in total are expected to be £108,000 and direct labour hours are planned to be 90,000 hours costing £5 per hour, what is the overhead absorption rate per direct labour hour?

(b) If production overheads in total are expected to be £720,000 and direct machine hours are planned to be 50,000 hours, what is the overhead absorption rate per direct machine hour?

6.3 The arbitrary nature of absorption costing

It should be obvious to you that, even if a company is trying to be 'fair', there is a great **lack of precision** about the way an absorption base is chosen.

This arbitrariness is one of the main criticisms of absorption costing, and if absorption costing is to be used then it is important that **the methods used are kept under regular review.** Changes in working conditions should, if necessary, lead to changes in the way in which work is accounted for.

For example, a **labour intensive department** may become **mechanised**. If a direct labour hour rate of absorption had been used previous to the mechanisation, it would probably now be more appropriate to change to the use of a machine hour rate.

7 Single factory-wide absorption rates and separate departmental absorption rates

7.1 Single factory-wide absorption rates

A **single factory-wide overhead absorption rate** is an absorption rate used throughout a factory for all jobs and units of output irrespective of the department in which they were produced. It is sometimes called a **blanket overhead absorption rate.**

Consider a factory in which total overheads were £500,000 and there were 250,000 machine hours, during a period. We could calculate a **single factory-wide overhead absorption rate** of £2 per machine hour (£500,000 ÷ 250,000). This would mean that all jobs passing through the factory would be **charged at the same rate** of £2 per machine hour.

The factory may have a number of departments undertaking different activities and jobs may not spend an equal amount of time in each department. In this situation the use of a **single factory-wide overhead absorption rate** is not really appropriate.

The main argument against the use of single factory-wide overhead absorption rates is the fact that **some products will absorb a higher overhead charge than is fair. Other products will absorb less overhead cost than is fair.**

If different departments use separate absorption rates **appropriate to the department's activity**, overheads should be charged to products on a **fairer basis** than when blanket overhead absorption rates are used. The overhead charged to products should then be **representative of the costs of the efforts and resources put into making them.**

7.2 Separate departmental absorption rates

Gibson Ltd has two production departments, for which the following budgeted information is available.

	Department Alpha	Department Beta	Total
Estimated overheads	£360,000	£200,000	£560,000
Estimated direct labour hours	200,000	40,000	240,000

If a single factory-wide overhead absorption rate per direct labour hour is applied, the factory-wide rate of overhead recovery would be:

$$\frac{£560,000}{240,000 \text{ hrs}} = £2.33 \text{ per direct labour hour}$$

If separate departmental overhead absorption rates are applied, these would be:

Department Alpha $= \dfrac{£360,000}{200,000 \text{ hours}}$ **Department Beta** $= \dfrac{£200,000}{40,000 \text{ hours}}$

$= £1.80$ per direct labour hour $= £5$ per direct labour hour

Department Beta has a higher overhead absorption rate per hour worked.

Activity 7.7

Le Toast Ltd make two types of toaster. One model is for domestic use selling for £400 and the other for industrial applications selling for £500. Unit costs are as follows.

	Domestic £	Industrial £
Direct materials	28	40
Direct labour	180	80
Direct expenses	40	200

Direct labour is paid at the rate of £10 per hour. Direct expenses comprise machine running costs and these are incurred at the rate of £8 per machine hour.

Production overheads in the coming year are expected to be £1,040,000. Planned production volume is 20,000 units of each product.

Task

Calculate the production overhead absorption rate and the total (direct and indirect) production cost per unit of each product if a single factory-wide overhead absorption rate per direct labour hour is used.

Helping hand. Use the information about labour cost per unit to derive the number of labour hours per unit, and hence the total forecast labour hours.

8 Over and under absorption

8.1 Predetermined recovery rates

It was stated earlier that the usual method of accounting for overheads is to add overhead costs on the basis of a **predetermined recovery rate**. This rate is a sort of **expected cost** since it is based on figures representing what is supposed to happen (that is, figures from the budget). Using the **predetermined overhead absorption rate**, the actual cost of production can be established as follows.

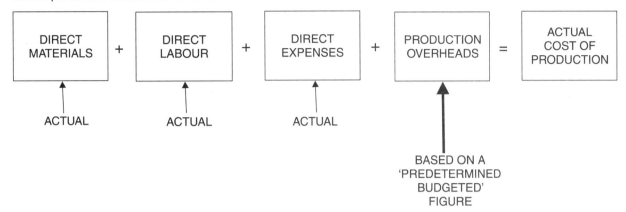

| DIRECT MATERIALS | + | DIRECT LABOUR | + | DIRECT EXPENSES | + | PRODUCTION OVERHEADS | = | ACTUAL COST OF PRODUCTION |

ACTUAL   ACTUAL   ACTUAL

BASED ON A 'PREDETERMINED BUDGETED' FIGURE

Many students become seriously confused about what can appear to be a very unusual method of costing (**actual cost** of production including a figure based on the **budget**). Study the following example. It will help to clarify this tricky point.

Example: Using the predetermined recovery rate

Fred Ltd budgeted to make 100 units of product called Ashley at a cost of £3 per unit in direct materials and £4 per unit in direct labour. The sales price would be £12 per unit, and production overheads were budgeted to amount to £200. A unit basis of overhead recovery is in operation. During the period 120 units were actually produced and sold (for £12 each) and the actual cost of direct materials was £380 and of direct labour, £450. Overheads incurred came to £210.

Task

Calculate the cost of sales and profit for product Ashley. Ignore administration, selling and distribution overheads.

Solution

The cost of production is the actual direct cost plus the cost of overheads, **absorbed at a predetermined rate** as established in the budget.

Overhead recovery rate = $\dfrac{£200}{100\,\text{units}}$ = £2 per unit produced.

The actual cost of sales of product Ashley is calculated as follows.

	£
Direct materials (actual)	380
Direct labour (actual)	450
Overheads absorbed (120 units × £2)	240
Full cost of sales	1,070
Sales value (120 units × £12)	1,440
Profit	370

8.2 Under/over absorption of overheads

You may already have noticed in the example above that **the actual overheads incurred**, £210, **are not the same as the overheads absorbed** (or included) into the cost of production. It is the overheads absorbed (£240) that will be debited to the profit and loss account. At the end of the accounting period an adjustment will need to be made in order to reflect the actual overheads of £210 that were incurred.

The discrepancy between actual overheads incurred, and the overheads absorbed is the **under absorption** or **over absorption** of overhead. This under/over absorption is an inevitable feature of absorption costing.

8.3 Why does under or over absorption occur?

The overhead absorption rate is predetermined from estimates of overhead cost and the expected volume of activity. It is quite likely, therefore, that either one or both of the estimates will not agree with what actually occurs. When this happens, under or over absorption of overheads will arise.

Example: Under/over absorption of overheads

The estimated overhead in a production department is £80,000 and the estimated activity is 40,000 direct labour hours. The overhead recovery rate (using a direct labour hour basis) would be £2 per direct labour hour (£80,000 ÷ 40,000 direct labour hours).

Actual overheads in the period are, say £84,000 and 45,000 direct labour hours are worked.

	£
Overhead incurred (actual)	84,000
Overhead absorbed (45,000 × £2)	90,000
Over absorption of overhead	6,000

In this example, the cost of units produced has been charged with £6,000 more than was actually spent. An adjustment to reconcile the overheads charged to the actual overhead is necessary and the over-absorbed overhead will be **written off as a credit in the profit and loss account** at the end of the accounting period.

Example: More under/over absorption of overheads

Uttoxeter Ltd has a budgeted production overhead of £50,000 and a budgeted activity of 25,000 direct labour hours and therefore a recovery rate of £2 per direct labour hour (£50,000 ÷ 25,000 direct labour hours). Calculate the under-/over-absorbed overhead, and explain the reasons for the under/over absorption, in the following circumstances.

(a) Actual overheads cost £47,000 and 25,000 direct labour hours are worked.
(b) Actual overheads cost £50,000 and 21,500 direct labour hours are worked.
(c) Actual overheads cost £47,000 and 21,500 direct labour hours are worked.

Solution

(a)

	£
Actual overhead	47,000
Absorbed overhead (25,000 × £2)	50,000
Over-absorbed overhead	3,000

Here there is **over absorption** because although the actual and estimated direct labour hours are the same, actual overheads cost *less* than expected and so too much overhead has been charged against profit.

(b)

	£
Actual overhead	50,000
Absorbed overhead (21,500 × £2)	43,000
Under-absorbed overhead	7,000

Here there is **under absorption** because although estimated and actual overhead costs were the same, fewer direct labour hours were worked than expected and hence insufficient overheads have been charged against profit.

(c)

	£
Actual overhead	47,000
Absorbed overhead (21,500 × £2)	43,000
Under-absorbed overhead	4,000

The reason for the net **under absorption** is a combination of the reasons in (a) and (b).

Activity 7.8

The actual total production overhead expenditure of Nuthatch Ltd, was £176,533. Its actual activity, and the predetermined overhead absorption rates were as follows.

	Machine shop A	Machine shop B	Assembly
Direct labour hours	8,200	6,500	21,900
Machine usage hours	7,300	18,700	-
Predetermined overhead absorption rates	£7.94 per machine hr	£3.50 per machine hr	£2.24 per direct labour hr

Task

Calculate the under or over absorption of overheads.

The following equation should help you to calculate the under/over absorption of overheads quickly and easily.

ACTUAL OVERHEADS – ABSORBED OVERHEADS = POSITIVE / NEGATIVE VALUE

- If the result is NEGATIVE (N), there is OVER ABSORPTION (O)
- If the result is POSITIVE (P), there is UNDER ABSORPTION (U)

Remember **NOPU!**

Key learning points

☑ **Overhead** is part of the cost incurred in the course of making a product, providing a service or running a department, which cannot be traced directly and in full to the product, service or department.

☑ The four main types of overhead are **production, administration, selling** and **distribution.**

☑ The objective of absorption costing is to include in the total cost of a product or service an appropriate share of the organisation's total overhead.

☑ **Allocation, apportionment** and **absorption** are the three steps of calculating the costs of overheads to be charged to manufactured output.

☑ **Apportionment** is a procedure whereby indirect costs (overheads) are spread fairly between cost centres.

☑ The **first stage of apportionment** is the **sharing out of common costs** using appropriate bases of apportionment.

☑ The **second stage of apportionment** is the apportionment of the service cost centre overheads to the production cost centres. This is sometimes called **reapportionment.**

☑ Service cost centre costs may be apportioned to production cost centres by the **direct method,** or the **step down method.**

☑ Overhead absorption is the process whereby costs of cost centres are added to unit, job or batch costs. Overhead absorption is sometimes called **overhead recovery.**

☑ **Predetermined overhead absorption** rates are calculated using budgeted figures. **Direct machine hour rates** are appropriate where production is controlled or dictated by machines. A **direct labour hour rate is** more appropriate in a labour intensive environment.

☑ There is a lack of precision about the way an absorption basis is chosen – the **arbitrary nature** of absorption costing is one of its main criticisms.

☑ The actual cost of production is made up of the following.

  – Direct materials
  – Direct labour
  – Direct expenses
  – Overheads (based on the predetermined overhead absorption rate)

☑ **A single factory-wide overhead absorption rate** (or **blanket overhead absorption rate)** is an absorption rate used throughout a factory for all jobs and units of output irrespective of the department in which they were produced. Sometimes it might be more appropriate to calculate **separate departmental absorption rates.**

☑ **Under** or **over absorption** of overheads occurs because the predetermined overhead absorption rates are based on forecasts (estimates).

☑ If actual overheads are greater than absorbed overheads, then overheads are **under absorbed.**

☑ If actual overheads are less than absorbed overheads, then overheads are **over absorbed.**

☑ The **NOPU** rule should help you to calculate under/over absorption of overheads quickly and easily.

ACTUAL OVERHEADS – ABSORBED OVERHEADS = POSITIVE / NEGATIVE VALUE

- If the result is NEGATIVE (N), there is OVER ABSORPTION (O)
- If the result is POSITIVE (P), there is UNDER ABSORPTION (U)

Quick quiz

1   What is allocation?

2   Match the following overheads with the most appropriate basis of apportionment.

Overhead		**Basis of apportionment**	
(a)	Depreciation of equipment	(1)	Direct machine hours
(b)	Heat and light costs	(2)	Number of employees
(c)	Canteen	(3)	Book value of equipment
(d)	Insurance of equipment	(4)	Floor area

3   Which of the following departments are directly involved in production?

Department	Involved in production (✓)
Finished goods warehouse Canteen Machining department Offices Assembly department	

4   In relation to calculating total absorption cost, label the following descriptions in the correct order as Steps 1 – 5.

Description	**Step**
A Apportion overhead costs between departments	
B Establish the overhead absorption rate	
C Choose fair methods of apportionment	
D Apply the overhead absorption rate to products	
E Reapportion service department costs	

5   How do the direct and step down methods of service cost centre apportionment differ?

6   A direct labour hour basis of overhead absorption is most appropriate in which of the following environments?

    A   Machine-intensive
    B   Labour-intensive
    C   When all units produced are identical
    D   None of the above

7   Does over absorption occur when absorbed overheads are greater than or less than actual overheads?

    ☐   Greater than

    ☐   Less than

8   Bridge Ltd has a budgeted production overhead of £214,981 and a budgeted activity of 35,950 hours of direct labour. Before settling on these estimates the company's accountant had a number of other possibilities for each figure, as shown below. Determine (preferably by inspection rather than full calculation) whether overheads will be over or under absorbed in each case if the alternatives turn out to be the actual figures.

Over or under absorption

(a) $\dfrac{£215,892}{35,950}$ ☐

(b) $\dfrac{£214,981}{36,005}$ ☐

(c) $\dfrac{£213,894}{36,271}$ ☐

(d) $\dfrac{£215,602}{35,440}$ ☐

Answers to quick quiz

1   The process whereby whole cost items are charged direct to a cost unit or cost centre.

2   (a)   (3)
        (b)   (4)
        (c)   (2)
        (d)   (3)

3

Department	Involved in production (✓)
Finished goods warehouse	
Canteen	
Machining department	✓
Offices	
Assembly department	✓

4   A = 2
        B = 4
        C = 1
        D = 5
        E = 3

5   The **direct method** is generally used when inter-service department work is not taken into account, ie the costs of each service cost centre are apportioned to production cost centres only.

The step down method involves the following.

- Apportioning one of the service cost centre's overheads to the cost centres using its services (production and service).

- Apportioning the overheads of the remaining service cost centre to the **production departments only.**

BPP
PROFESSIONAL EDUCATION

6   B

7 | ✓ | Greater than

8   **Helping hand.** You could try to answer this activity by considering how the value of a simple fraction like 4 divided by 2 would increase or decrease as the value of the denominator or numerator varied. Remember that if the actual rate is more than the estimated rate there will be under absorption and vice versa.

(a)   Under (because actual production overheads are higher than estimated).
(b)   Over (because actual hours are higher than estimated).
(c)   Over (because actual production overheads are lower than estimated and actual hours are higher).
(d)   Under (because actual hours are lower than estimated and actual hours are higher).

Helping hand. If you find it difficult to do this by inspection, there is nothing wrong with calculating the estimated rate (£214,981 ÷ 35,950 hours = £5.98) and then the actual rate in each case (£6.00; £5.97; £5.90; £6.08), but having done this make sure that you can explain in non-numerical terms what has happened. For example, in (c) lower overheads and a higher number of active hours have led to over absorption.

chapter 8

Bookkeeping entries for cost information

Contents

1 Introduction

You should now have a good idea of the way that the materials, labour and overhead costs of an item are determined. Now it is time to see how the costs and revenues are recorded **in total** in the cost accounting **bookkeeping system.**

2 Cost information and ledger accounting

In previous chapters we have scrupulously avoided T accounts, debits and credits, ledgers and bookkeeping. The cost records we have described so far are quite adequate for individual products or jobs, and it is not essential to go beyond this.

However, unless records of **totals** are maintained and checks of these records are made, there is no way of knowing whether all the costs that should have been recorded really have been recorded. The solution to this problem is **to link the cost records to the cash and credit transactions that are summarised in the main ledger**. If you like you can think of recording cost information as dealing with debits. Let us look at an example to illustrate what we mean.

Examples: Cost information and ledger accounting

(a) Suppose you buy £100 of materials for cash and £100 on credit. What entries will you make in the ledgers?

(b) From the knowledge you have already acquired elsewhere you should have no difficulty in answering this question. The cash transaction will be recorded in the cash book, analysed as appropriate. It will also be recorded in the main ledger as follows.

		£	£
DEBIT	Purchases	100	
CREDIT	Cash		100

(c) The credit transaction will be recorded in the purchase ledger under the name of the supplier in question. It will also be recorded in the main ledger as follows.

		£	£
DEBIT	Purchases	100	
CREDIT	Creditors ledger control account		100

(d) Now consider this transaction from the point of view of what you have learnt in this Interactive Text. The appropriate **stores record card** and **bin card** will have been updated to show the acquisition of £200 worth of stock but the cash and credit side of the transactions have not entered any cost records. In other words, the cost records are only interested in the entry made in the main ledger under purchases.

We could go further and explain that just as the analysed cash book is a very detailed breakdown of the entries in the cash control account in the main ledger, and just as the creditors ledger shows the detailed information behind the creditors ledger control account, **the cost records are a detailed breakdown of the information contained in the purchases account, the wages and salaries account, and all the expense accounts in the main ledger.**

It is tempting to go no further than this. So long as you understand the basic principles of double entry bookkeeping, the cost accounting aspects of it should cause you no more difficulty than any other aspects.

All you really need to know, however, is the following.

- How to turn purchases, wages and so on into finished units of production
- How to deal with under- or over-absorbed overheads

3 Getting costs into finished units

3.1 Materials

First, let's look at how a single purchase of materials works through into the final accounts. The relevant double entries are as follows.

			£	£
(a)	DEBIT	Materials	X	
	CREDIT	Cash		X

Being the buying of materials which are put into raw materials stock

			£	£
(b)	DEBIT	Work in progress	X	
	CREDIT	Materials stock		X

Being the issue of materials to production for use in work in progress

			£	£
(c)	DEBIT	Finished goods	X	
	CREDIT	Work in progress		X

Being the issue of units that are now finished to finished goods stock

			£	£
(d)	DEBIT	Cost of sales	X	
	CREDIT	Finished goods		X

Being the taking of units out of finished goods stock and selling them

			£	£
(e)	DEBIT	Profit and loss account	X	
	CREDIT	Cost of sales		X

Being the closing off of ledger accounts and the drawing up of financial statements. This entry would only be made at the end of a period.

Examples: Basic cost accounting entries for materials

Fred Flintstone Ltd begins trading with £200 cash. £200 is initially spent on timber to make garden furniture. £100 worth of timber is left in store, while the other £100 is worked on to make garden chairs and tables. Before long, £50 worth of timber has been converted into garden furniture and this furniture is sold for £150. How will these events and transactions be reflected in the accounts?

Solution

CASH ACCOUNT

	£		£
Cash - opening balance	200	Purchase of materials	200
Sale of finished goods-sales	150	Closing balance	150
	350		350

MATERIALS ACCOUNT

	£		£
Cash purchase	200	Transfer to WIP	100
		Closing balance	100
	200		200

WORK IN PROGRESS ACCOUNT

	£		£
Transfer from materials	100	Transfer to finished goods	50
		Closing balance	50
	100		100

FINISHED GOODS ACCOUNT

	£		£
Transfer from WIP	50	Transfer to cost of sales	50
	50		50

COST OF SALES ACCOUNT

	£		£
Transfer from finished goods	50	Shown in profit and loss account	50
	50		50

SALES ACCOUNT

	£		£
Shown in profit and loss account	150	Cash	150
	150		150

FRED FLINTSTONE LTD
PROFIT AND LOSS ACCOUNT

	£
Sales	150
Cost of sales	50
Profit	100

3.2 Accounting for labour costs

We will use an example to review briefly the principal bookkeeping entries for wages.

Examples: The wages control account

The following details were extracted from a weekly payroll for 750 employees at a factory in Trinidad.

Analysis of gross wages

	Direct workers £	Indirect workers £	Total £
Ordinary time	36,000	22,000	58,000
Overtime: basic wage	8,700	5,430	14,130
premium	4,350	2,715	7,065
Shift allowance	3,465	1,830	5,295
Sick pay	950	500	1,450
Idle time	3,200	-	3,200
Total gross wages	56,665	32,475	89,140
Net wages paid to employees	£45,605	£24,220	£69,825

Task

Prepare the wages control account for the week.

Solution

(a) **The wages control account** acts as a sort of **collecting place** for net wages paid and deductions made from gross pay. The gross pay is then analysed between **direct** and **indirect wages**.

(b) The first step is to determine which wage costs are **direct** and which are **indirect**. The direct wages will be debited to the **work in progress account** and the indirect wages will be debited to the **production overhead account**.

(c) There are in fact only two items of direct wages cost in this example, the ordinary time (£36,000) and the basic overtime wage (£8,700) paid to direct workers. All other payments (including the overtime premium) are indirect wages.

(d) The net wages paid are debited to the control account, and the balance then represents the deductions which have been made for income tax, national insurance, and so on.

WAGES CONTROL ACCOUNT

	£		£
		Work in progress:	
Bank: net wages paid	69,825	direct labour	44,700
		Production overhead control:	
Deductions control accounts*		indirect labour	27,430
(£89,140 – £69,825)	19,315	Overtime premium	7,065
		Shift allowance	5,295
		Sick pay	1,450
		Idle time	3,200

89,140   89,140

* In practice there would be a separate deductions control account for each type of deduction made (for example, PAYE and National Insurance).

Activity 8.1

What items are included in a wages control account?

4 Control accounts

4.1 Control accounts

A **control account** is an account which records total cost. In contrast, individual ledger accounts record individual debits and credits.

Obviously the previous section is highly simplified. This is to avoid obscuring the basic principles. For example, we have until now assumed that if £200 of materials are purchased the only entries made will be Dr Materials, Cr Cash. In practice, of course, this £200 might be made up of 20 different types of material, each costing £10, and if so each type of material is likely to have its own sub-account.

These sub-accounts would be exactly like individual personal accounts in the creditors' ledger or the debtors' ledger. You have probably guessed that we need to use **control accounts** to summarise the detailed transactions (such as how the £200 of materials is made up) and to maintain the double entry in the main ledger.

- A **materials control account** (or **stores control account**) records the total cost of invoices received for each type of material (purchases) and the total cost of each type of material issued to various departments (the sum of the value of all materials requisition notes).

- A **wages control account** records the total cost of the payroll (plus employer's national insurance contributions) and the total cost of direct and indirect labour as recorded in the wages analysis sheets and charged to each production unit, job, or batch.

- A **production overhead control account** is a total record of actual expenditure incurred and the amount absorbed into individual units, jobs or batches. Subsidiary records for actual overhead expenditure items and cost records which show the overheads attributed to individual units or jobs must agree with or reconcile to the totals in the control account.

- A **work in progress control account** records the total costs of direct materials, direct wages and production overheads charged to units, jobs or batches, and the cost of finished goods which are completed and transferred to the distribution department. Subsidiary records of individual job costs and so on will exist for jobs still in production and for jobs completed.

Activity 8.2

The following data relate to the stores ledger control account of Fresh Ltd, an air freshener manufacturer, for the month of April 20X0.

	£
Opening stock	18,500
Closing stock	16,100
Deliveries from suppliers	142,000
Returns to suppliers	2,300
Cost of indirect materials issued	25,200

Tasks

(a)   Calculate the value of the issue of direct materials during April 20X0.
(b)   State the double entry to record the issue of direct materials in the cost accounts.

5 Cost bookkeeping systems

There are two types of cost bookkeeping system, the **interlocking** and the **integrated.** Interlocking systems require **separate ledgers** to be kept for the cost accounting function and the financial accounting function, which means that the cost accounting profit and financial accounting profit have to be **reconciled**. Integrated systems, on the other hand, **combine the two functions in one set of ledger accounts.**

Modern cost accounting systems (computerised) integrate cost accounting information and financial accounting information and are known as **integrated systems.** You are much more likely to deal with integrated systems, and this is the system we shall be looking at in detail.

5.1 Integrated systems

An **integrated system** is a system where the cost accounting function and the financial accounting function are combined in one system of ledger accounts.

The following diagram shows a cost accounting system which uses absorption costing. The entries in the individual accounts have been simplified. Study the diagram carefully, and work through the double entries represented in the diagram. **Make sure that you understand the logic behind the flow of costs**.

Cost accounting using absorption costing

5.2 Dealing with overheads

When an absorption costing system is in use, we know that the amount of overhead included in the cost of an item is **absorbed at a predetermined rate.** The entries made in the cash book and the main ledger, however, are the **actual amounts**.

As we saw in an earlier chapter, it is highly unlikely that the actual amount and the predetermined amount will be the same. The difference is called **under- or over-absorbed overhead**. To deal with this in the cost accounting books we need to have an account to collect under- or over-absorbed amounts for each type of overhead.

Example: The under-/over-absorbed overhead account

Gnocci Ltd absorbs production overheads at the rate of £0.50 per operating hour and administration overheads at 20% of the production cost of sales. Actual data for one month was as follows.

Administration overheads	£32,000
Production overheads	£46,500
Operating hours	90,000
Production cost of sales	£180,000

What entries need to be made for overheads in the ledgers?

Solution

PRODUCTION OVERHEAD CONTROL ACCOUNT

	£		£
Cash	46,500	Absorbed into WIP(90,000 × £0.50)	45,000
		Under-absorbed overhead	1,500
	46,500		46,500

ADMINISTRATION OVERHEAD CONTROL ACCOUNT

	£		£
Cash	32,000	To cost of sales (£180,000 × 0.2)	36,000
Over-absorbed overhead	4,000		
	36,000		36,000

UNDER-/OVER-ABSORBED OVERHEAD ACCOUNT

	£		£
Production overhead	1,500	Administration overhead	4,000
Balance to profit and loss a/c	2,500		
	4,000		4,000

Less production overhead has been absorbed than has been spent so there is **under-absorbed production overhead of £1,500**. More administration overhead has been absorbed (into cost of sales, note, not into WIP) and so there is **over-absorbed administration overhead of £4,000**. The net over-absorbed overhead of £2,500 is a **credit in the profit and loss account.**

Activity 8.3

PO Ltd absorbs production overheads using a direct labour hour rate. Data for last period are as follows.

Production overheads incurred – paid through bank account	£125,478
Depreciation of production machinery	£4,100
Direct labour hours worked	27,000
Production overhead absorption rate per direct labour hour	£5

Task

Prepare the production overhead control account for the period.

Example: Integrated accounts

Shown below are the opening balances for the month of September 20X0 for Vermicelli Ltd, with a summary bank account and information obtained from the stores department, the payroll department and the production department. The provisions for depreciation are also given below. During the month goods costing £196,000 were sold (all on credit) for £278,000.

OPENING BALANCES - SEPTEMBER 20X0

	Dr	Cr
	£'000	£'000
Raw materials stores account	30	
Work in progress account	20	
Finished goods account	60	
Debtors account	74	
Creditors account		85
Creditors for National Insurance & PAYE		19
Factory buildings account	250	
Provision for depreciation: factory buildings		20
Equipment account	320	
Provision for depreciation: equipment		170
Share capital account		100
Share premium account		20
Profit and loss reserve		290
Cash and bank account		50
	754	754

STORES REPORT - SEPTEMBER 20X0

	£'000
Materials received from suppliers and invoiced	40
Materials issued to production	32
Materials issued to production service departments	8
Materials issued to administrative departments	2

PROFESSIONAL EDUCATION

PAYROLL REPORT - SEPTEMBER 20X0

	Gross wages £'000	PAYE & employees' NI £'000	Net £'000	Employer's NI £'000
Direct wages (£5.50 per hour)	33	8	25	2
Production indirect wages	7	1	6	-
Administrative staff wages and salaries	10	3	7	1
Selling staff wages and salaries	10	3	7	1
	60	15	45	4

PRODUCTION REPORT - SEPTEMBER 20X0

Production overhead absorption rate	£12.50 per direct labour hour
Cost of work completed in the month	£150,000

CASH AND BANK ACCOUNT

	£'000		£'000
Debtors	290	Balance b/f	50
		Wages and salaries	45
		Production overhead	15
		Administration overhead	8
		Selling overhead	20
		Creditor for national insurance and PAYE	19
		Creditors	45
		Balance c/f (surplus)	88
	290		290
Balance b/f	88		

PROVISIONS FOR DEPRECIATION - SEPTEMBER 20X0

	£'000
Factory buildings	2
Factory equipment	35
Office equipment	5
	42

Tasks

(a)   Post the information given in the example to the integrated accounts of Vermicelli Ltd.

(b)   Prepare a trial balance for Vermicelli Ltd, as at 30 September 20X0.

(c)   Prepare a trading and profit loss account for Vermicelli Ltd for September 20X0.

Solution

(a)

RAW MATERIALS STORES ACCOUNT

	£'000		£'000
Balance b/f	30	Work in progress account	32
Creditors	40	Production overhead account	8
		Administration overhead account	2
		Balance c/f	28
	70		70
Balance b/f	28		

WAGES AND SALARIES ACCOUNT

	£'000		£'000
Bank	45	Work in progress	33
Creditor for national insurance and PAYE	15	Production overhead	7
		Administration overhead	10
		Selling overhead	10
	60		60

PRODUCTION OVERHEAD ACCOUNT

	£'000		£'000
Raw materials stores	8	Work in progress (note 1)	75
Wages and salaries	7		
Bank (expenses)	15		
Depreciation: buildings	2		
Depreciation: equipment	35		
Over-absorbed overhead to P + L	8		
	75		75

WORK IN PROGRESS ACCOUNT

	£'000		£'000
Balance b/f	20	Finished goods	150
Raw materials stores	32		
Wages and salaries	33		
Creditor for national insurance	2		
Production overhead	75	Balance c/f	12
	162		162
Balance b/f	12		

FINISHED GOODS ACCOUNT

	£'000		£'000
Balance b/f	60	Cost of sales	196
Work in progress	150	Balance c/f	14
	210		210
Balance b/f	14		

COST OF SALES ACCOUNT

	£'000		£'000
Finished goods	196	Profit and loss account	196

ADMINISTRATION OVERHEAD ACCOUNT

	£'000		£'000
Raw materials stores	2	Profit and loss account	
Wages and salaries	10	(note 2)	26
Bank (expenses)	8		
Creditor for national insurance	1		
Depreciation	5		
	26		26

SELLING OVERHEAD ACCOUNT

	£'000		£'000
Wages and salaries	10	Profit and loss account	31
Bank (expenses)	20		
Creditor for national insurance	1		
	31		31

SALES ACCOUNT

	£'000		£'000
Profit and loss account	278	Debtors	278

TRADING AND PROFIT AND LOSS ACCOUNT

	£'000		£'000
Cost of sales	196	Sales	278
Gross profit c/d	82		
	278		278
Administration overhead	26	Gross profit b/d	82
Selling overhead	31	Over-absorbed overhead	8
Profit and loss reserve	33		
	90		90

DEBTORS ACCOUNT

	£'000		£'000
Balance b/f	74	Bank	290
Sales	278	Balance c/f	62
	352		352
Balance b/f	62		

CREDITORS ACCOUNT

	£'000		£'000
Bank	45	Balance b/f	85
Balance c/f	80	Raw materials stores	40
	125		125
		Balance b/f	80

CREDITORS FOR NATIONAL INSURANCE & PAYE

	£'000		£'000
Bank	19	Balance b/f	19
		Wages and salaries	15
Balance c/f	19	Employer's contributions:	
		Work in progress	2
		Administration overhead	1
		Selling overhead	1
	38		38
		Balance b/f	19

FACTORY BUILDINGS ACCOUNT

	£'000		£'000
Balance b/f	250	Balance c/f	250

PROVISION FOR DEPRECIATION: FACTORY BUILDINGS

	£'000		£'000
Balance c/f	22	Balance b/f	20
		Charge for September 20X0	2
	22		22
		Balance b/f	22

EQUIPMENT ACCOUNT

	£'000		£'000
Balance b/f	320	Balance c/f	320

PROVISION FOR DEPRECIATION: EQUIPMENT

	£'000		£'000
Balance c/f	210	Balance b/f	170
		Factory equipment charge	35
		Office equipment charge	5
	210		210
		Balance b/f	210

SHARE CAPITAL ACCOUNT

	£'000		£'000
Balance c/f	100	Balance b/f	100

SHARE PREMIUM ACCOUNT

	£'000		£'000
Balance c/f	20	Balance b/f	20

PROFIT AND LOSS RESERVE

	£'000		£'000
Balance c/f	323	Balance b/f	290
		Profit and loss account	33
	323		323
		Balance b/f	323

(b) The trial balance as at 30 September 20X0 is as follows.

	DR £'000		CR £'000
Raw materials stores	28	Creditors	80
Work in progress	12	Creditor for national insurance	
Finished goods	14	and PAYE	19
Cash and bank	88	Provision for depreciation:	
Debtors	62	Factory buildings	22
Factory buildings	250	Equipment	210
Equipment	320	Share capital	100
		Share premium	20
		Profit and loss reserve	323
	774		774

Notes

(1) The amount of production overhead absorbed into WIP is calculated by multiplying the rate given (£12.50 per direct labour hour) by the number of direct labour hours, which was £33,000/£5.50 = 6,000.

£12.50 × 6,000 = £75,000

(2) We are not told that administration and selling overheads are absorbed into units produced, so we must assume that the actual costs are charged in full in the period in which they are incurred. A 'vertical' profit and loss account may make this clearer.

(c) VERMICELLI LTD PROFIT & LOSS ACCOUNT
30 SEPTEMBER 20X0

	£'000	£'000
Sales		278
Opening stocks (30 + 20 + 60)	110	
Direct materials purchased (40 – 8 – 2)	30	
Wages and salaries (33 + 2)	35	
Production overhead absorbed	75	
	250	
Closing stocks (28 + 12 + 14)	(54)	
Cost of sales		196
Gross profit		82
Administration overhead	26	
Selling overhead	31	
Over-absorbed overhead	(8)	
		(49)
Net profit		33

Activity 8.4

What would be the double entry to record the following events in an integrated accounts system?

(a)   Materials costing £10,000 are purchased on credit and put into stock.
(b)   Finished units costed at £50,000 are made available for sale.
(c)   Materials valued at £5,000 are issued to the administration department.
(d)   Indirect production wages of £20,000 are charged to the production department.

Activity 8.5

In the absence of the accountant you have been asked to prepare a month's cost accounts for Liverpool Ltd, a company which operates a costing system which is fully **integrated** with the financial accounts. The cost clerk has provided you with the following information.

(a)   *Balances at beginning of month*

	£
Stores ledger control account	24,175
Work in progress control account	19,210
Finished goods control account	34,164
Creditors control account	15,187

(b)   *Information relating to events during the month*

	£
Materials purchased	76,150
Materials issued from stores to production	29,630
Gross wages paid: direct workers	15,236
indirect workers	9,462
Payments to creditors	58,320
Selling and distribution overheads incurred	5,240
Other production overheads incurred but not yet paid for	16,300
Sales	75,400
Cost of finished goods sold	59,830
Cost of goods completed and transferred into finished goods store during the month	62,130

(c)   *The production overhead absorption rate is 150% of direct wages.*

Task

Prepare the following accounts for the month:

Stores ledger control account	Production overhead control account
Work in progress control account	Creditors control account
Finished goods control account	Profit and loss account

Key learning points

☑ A **control account** is an account which records total cost, unlike an individual ledger account which records individual debits and credits.

☑ There are two main types of cost bookkeeping system, **interlocking systems** and **integrated systems**.

☑ An **integrated system** is one in which the cost accounting function and the financial accounting function are combined in one system of ledger accounts.

☑ The **wages control account** acts as a collecting place for wages before they are analysed into work in progress and production overhead control accounts.

☑ The **production overhead control account** acts as a collecting place for production overheads before they are absorbed into work in progress.

☑ Production overhead is absorbed into work in progress using the **predetermined overhead absorption rate**.

☑ Any balance remaining on the production overhead control account at the end of the period represents the **overhead under or over absorbed** during the period.

Quick quiz

1   What is a control account?

2   What are the two types of cost bookkeeping system?

3   What is the double entry for indirect materials issued to production?

4   What does it mean if the debit total on the production overhead control account is higher than the credit total?

Answers to quick quiz

1   An account which records total cost, as opposed to individual costs (which are recorded in individual ledger accounts).

2   Integrated and interlocking.

3   Debit Production overhead control account; Credit Materials stock account

4   Production overhead is under-absorbed.

chapter 9

Costing methods

Contents

1 Introduction

In this chapter we will be looking at two important costing methods: **job costing and batch costing.** These costing methods apply, as we discussed in Chapter 3, in situations where an organisation's output consists of separately identifiable units.

Job costing and batch costing systems can be distinguished from **unit costing systems,** as we saw in Chapter 3, because the latter apply when production consists of a continuous flow of identical units.

2 What is a costing method?

A **costing method** is a method of collecting costs which is designed to suit the way goods are processed or manufactured or the way that services are provided.

Each organisation's costing method will have unique features but **costing methods of firms in the same line of business will have common aspects.** On the other hand, organisations involved in completely different activities, such as hospitals and car part manufacturers, will use very different costing methods.

3 Job costing

The aim of **job costing** is simply to collect the cost information shown below.

	£
Direct materials	X
Direct labour	X
Direct expenses	X
Direct cost	X
Production overhead	X
Total production cost	X
Administration overhead	X
Selling overhead	X
Cost of sales	X

To the final figure is added a **'mark-up'** and the total is the selling price of the job.

In other words, all we are doing is looking at one way of putting together the pieces of information that we have studied separately so far.

3.1 What is a job?

A **job** is a cost unit which consists of a single order or contract.

With other methods of costing it is usual to produce for stock. Management therefore decide in advance how many units of each type, size, colour, quality and so on will be produced during the coming period.

These decisions will all be taken without taking into account the identity of the individual customers who will eventually buy the products.

In job costing on the other hand, production is usually carried out in accordance with the **special requirements** of each customer. It is therefore usual for each job to **differ in one or more respects from every other job**, which means that a separate record must be maintained to show the details of a particular job.

The work relating to a job is usually carried out within a factory or workshop and moves through processes and operations as a **continuously identifiable unit**. The term job may also be applied to work such as **property repairs**, and the job costing method may be used in the costing of **internal capital expenditure jobs** and **internal services**.

3.2 Procedure for the performance of jobs

The normal procedure in jobbing concerns involves the following.

(a)   The prospective customer approaches the supplier and indicates the **requirements** of the job.

(b)   A responsible official sees the prospective customer and agrees the **precise details of the items** to be supplied, for example the quantity, quality and colour of the goods, the date of delivery and any special requirements.

(c)   The estimating department of the organisation then prepares an **estimate** for the job. This will include the following.

- The cost of the materials to be used
- The wages expected to be paid
- The amount for factory, administration, selling and distribution overhead
- The cost of any additional equipment needed specially for the job
- The supplier's profit margin

The total of these items will represent the **quoted selling price**.

(d)   At the appropriate time, the job will be **'loaded'** on to the factory floor. This means that as soon as all materials, labour and equipment are available and subject to the scheduling of other orders, the job will be started. In an efficient organisation, **the start of the job will be timed to ensure that while it will be ready for the customer by the promised date of delivery it will not be loaded too early.** Otherwise storage space will have to be found for the product until the date it is required by the customer.

3.3 Collection of job costs

Each job will be given a **number** to identify it. A separate record must be maintained to show the details of individual jobs. The process of collecting job costs may be outlined as follows.

(a)   **Materials requisitions are sent to stores.**

(b)   **The materials requisition note will be used to cost the materials issued to the job** concerned, and this cost may then be recorded on a **job cost sheet**. The cost may include items already in stock, at an appropriate valuation, and/or items specially purchased.

(c)   **The job ticket is passed to the worker who is to perform the first operation**. The times of starting and finishing the operation are recorded on the ticket, which is then passed to the person who is to carry out the second operation, where a similar record of the times of starting and finishing is made.

(d) When the job is completed, the **job ticket is sent to the cost office**, where the time spent will be costed and recorded on the job cost sheet.

(e) The **relevant costs** of materials issued, direct labour performed and direct expenses incurred as recorded on the job cost sheet **are charged to the job account** in the work in progress ledger.

(f) **The job account is debited with the job's share of the factory overhead**, based on the absorption rate(s) in operation. If the job is incomplete at the end of an accounting period, it is valued at production cost in the closing balance sheet (where a system of absorption costing is in operation).

(g) **On completion of the job**, the job account is charged with the appropriate administration, selling and distribution overhead, after which **the total cost of the job can be ascertained.**

(h) The difference between the agreed selling price and the total actual cost will be the supplier's profit (or loss).

Here is a proforma job account, which will be one of the accounts in the work in progress control account.

JOB ACCOUNT

	£		£
Materials issued	X	Finished jobs	X
Direct labour	X		
Direct expenses	X		
Production overhead at predetermined rate	X		
Other overheads	X		X
	X		X

Activity 9.1

What does the word 'job' mean when we talk about job costing? Give three examples.

3.4 Job cost sheet (or card)

An example of a job cost sheet is shown below.

When jobs are completed, **job cost sheets** are transferred from the **work in progress** category to **finished goods**. When delivery is made to the customer, the costs become a **cost of sale**. If the completed job was carried out in order to build up finished goods stocks (rather than to meet a specific order) the quantity of items produced and their value are recorded on **finished goods stores ledger cards**.

JOB COST CARD

| | Job No. | B641 |

Customer	Mr J White
Customer's Order No.	
Vehicle make	Peugot 205 GTE
Job Description	Repair damage to offside front door
Vehicle reg. no.	G 614 SOX
Estimate Ref.	2599
Invoice No.	
Quoted price	£338.68
Invoice price	£355.05
Date to collect	14.6.X0

Material

Date	Req. No.	Qty.	Price	Cost £	Cost p
12.6	36815	1	75.49	75	49
12.6	36816	1	33.19	33	19
12.6	36842	5	6.01	30	05
13.6	36881	5	3.99	19	95
Total C/F				**158**	**68**

Labour

Date	Employee	Cost Ctre	Hrs.	Rate	Bonus	Cost £	Cost p
12.6	018	B	1.98	6.50	–	12	87
13.6	018	B	5.92	6.50	–	38	48
					13.65	13	65
Total C/F						**65**	**00**

Overheads

Hrs	OAR	Cost £	Cost p
7.9	2.50	19	75
Total C/F		**19**	**75**

Expenses

Date	Ref.	Description	Cost £	Cost p
12.6	–	N. Jolley Panel-beating	50	–
Total C/F			**50**	**–**

Job Cost Summary

	Actual £	Actual p	Estimate £	Estimate p
Direct Materials B/F	158	68	158	68
Direct Expenses B/F	50	00		
Direct Labour B/F	65	00	180	00
Direct Cost	273	68		
Overheads B/F	19	75		
	293	43		
Admin overhead (add 10%)	29	34		
= Total Cost	322	77	338	68
Invoice Price	355	05		
Job Profit/Loss	32	28		

Comments

Job Cost Card Completed by _

3.5 Job costing and computerisation

Job cost cards exist in **manual** systems, but it is increasingly likely that in large organisations the job costing system will be **computerised**, using accounting software specifically designed to deal with job costing requirements. A computerised job accounting system is likely to contain the following features.

(a) Every job will be given a **job code number**, which will determine how the data relating to the job is stored.

(b) A **separate set of codes** will be given for the type of costs that any job is likely to incur. Thus, 'direct wages', say, will have the same code whichever job they are allocated to.

(c) In a sophisticated system, **costs can be analysed both by job** (for example all costs related to Job 456), **and by type** (for example direct wages incurred on all jobs). It is thus easy to compare actual and expected costs and to make comparisons between jobs.

(d) A job costing system might have facilities built into it which incorporate other factors relating to the performance of the job. In complex jobs, sophisticated planning techniques might be employed to ensure that the job is performed in the minimum time possible. **Time management features** therefore may be incorporated into job costing software.

Activity 9.2

Three of the following documents were used to establish the direct costs of job C1027. Identify the documents in question.

Stock card 8754/1262
Payroll (week-ending 26 September 20X0)
Factory electricity bill for the quarter to 29 September 20X0
GRN No 45725
M Bobb's clock card (w/e 26 September 20X0)
Materials requisition note no 20019
Industrial Refuse Ltd - weekly invoices for skip hire
M Bobb's time sheet (w/e 26 September 20X0)
Fred Davis - invoice for sub-contracting work 'per quotation'

4 Job costing for internal services

Job costing systems may be used to control the costs of **internal service departments**, eg the maintenance department. A job costing system enables the cost of a specific job to be charged to a user department. Therefore instead of apportioning the total costs of service departments, each job done is charged to the individual user department.

An **internal job costing system** for service departments will have the following advantages.

(a) **Realistic apportionment**. The identification of expenses with jobs and the subsequent charging of these to the department(s) responsible means that costs are borne by those who incurred them.

(b) **Increased responsibility and awareness**. User departments will be aware that they are charged for the specific services used and may be more careful to use the facility more efficiently. They will also appreciate the true cost of the facilities that they are using and can take decisions accordingly.

(c) **Control of service department costs**. The service department may be restricted to charging a standard cost to user departments for specific jobs carried out or time spent. It will then be possible to measure the efficiency or inefficiency of the service department by recording the difference between the standard charges and the actual expenditure.

(d) **Budget information**. This information will ease the budgeting process, as the purpose and cost of service department expenditure can be separately identified.

Activity 9.3

East and West Ltd is a company that carries out jobbing work. One of the jobs carried out in May was job 2409, to which the following information relates.

Direct material Y:	400 kilos were issued from stores at a cost of £5 per kilo.
Direct material Z:	800 kilos were issued from stores at a cost of £6 per kilo. 60 kilos were returned.
Department P:	300 labour hours were worked, of which 100 hours were overtime.
Department Q:	200 labour hours were worked, of which 100 hours were overtime.

Overtime work is not normal in Department P, where basic pay is £4 per hour plus an overtime premium of £1 per hour. Overtime work was done in Department Q in May because of a request by the customer of another job to complete his job quickly. Basic pay in Department Q is £5 per hour and overtime premium is £1.50 per hour. Overhead is absorbed at the rate of £3 per direct labour hour in both departments.

Tasks

(a) Calculate the direct materials cost of job 2409
(b) Calculate the direct labour cost of job 2409
(c) Calculate the full production cost of job 2409 using absorption costing

Activity 9.4

A curtain-making business manufactures quality curtains to customers' orders. It has three production departments (X, Y and Z) which have overhead absorption rates (per direct labour hour) of £12.86, £12.40 and £14.03 respectively.

Two pairs of curtains are to be manufactured for customers. Direct costs are as follows.

	Job TN8	Job KT2
Direct material	£154	£108
Direct labour	20 hours dept X	16 hours dept X
	12 hours dept Y	10 hours dept Y
	10 hours dept Z	14 hours dept Z

Labour rates are as follows: £3.80(X); £3.50 (Y); £3.40 (Z)

The firm quotes prices to customers that reflect a required profit of 25% on selling price.

Task

Calculate the total cost and selling price of each job.

5 Batch costing

A **batch** is a cost unit which consists of a separate, readily identifiable group of product units which maintain their separate identity throughout the production process.

The procedures for **costing batches** are very similar to those for costing jobs.

(a) The batch is treated as a **job** during production and the costs are collected in the manner already described in this chapter.

(b) Once the batch has been completed, the **cost per unit** can be calculated as the total batch cost divided by the number of units in the batch.

Example: Control accounts

A company manufactures model cars to order and has the following budgeted overheads for the year, based on normal activity levels.

Department	Budgeted overheads £	Budgeted activity
Welding	6,000	1,500 labour hours
Assembly	10,000	1,000 labour hours

Selling and administrative overheads are 20% of production cost. An order for 250 model cars type XJS1, made as Batch 8638, incurred the following costs.

Materials	£12,000
Labour	100 hours welding shop at £2.50/hour
	200 hours assembly shop at £1/hour

£500 was paid for the hire of special X-ray equipment for testing the welds.

Task

Calculate the cost per unit for Batch 8638.

Solution

The first step is to calculate the overhead absorption rate for the production departments.

Welding $= \dfrac{£6,000}{1,500} =$ £4 per labour hour

Assembly $= \dfrac{£10,000}{1,000} =$ £10 per labour hour

			Total cost - Batch no 8638	
			£	£
Direct material				12,000
Direct expense				500
Direct labour	$100 \times 2.50 =$		250	
	$200 \times 1.00 =$		200	
				450
Prime cost				12,950
Overheads	$100 \times 4 =$		400	
	$200 \times 10 =$		2,000	
				2,400
Production cost				15,350
Selling and administrative cost (20% of production cost)				3,070
Total cost				18,420

Cost per unit $= \dfrac{£18,420}{250} = £73.68$

Activity 9.5

Lyfsa Kitchen Units Ltd crafts two different sizes of standard unit and a DIY all-purpose unit for filling up awkward spaces. The units are built to order in batches of around 250 (although the number varies according to the quality of wood purchased), and each batch is sold to NGJ Furniture Warehouses Ltd.

The costs incurred in May were as follows.

	Big unit	Little unit	All-purpose
Direct materials purchased	£5,240	£6,710	£3,820
Direct labour			
Skilled (hours)	1,580	1,700	160
Semi-skilled (hours)	3,160	1,900	300
Direct expenses	£1,180	£1,700	£250
Selling price of batch	£33,180	£27,500	£19,500
Completed at 31 May	100%	80%	25%

The following information is available.

All direct materials for the completion of the batches have been recorded. Skilled labour is paid £5 per hour, semi-skilled £4 per hour. Administration expenses total £4,400 per month and are to be allocated to the batches on the basis of direct labour hours. Direct labour costs, direct expenses and administration expenses will increase in proportion to the total labour hours required to complete the little units and the all-purpose units. On completion of the work the practice of the manufacturer is to divide the calculated profit on each batch 20% to staff as a bonus, 80% to the company. Losses are absorbed 100% by the company.

Tasks

(a) Calculate the profit or loss made by the company on big units.
(b) Project the profit or loss likely to be made by the company on little units and all-purpose units.
(c) Comment on any matters you think relevant to management as a result of your calculations.

Key learning points

☑ **Job costing** is the costing method used where each cost unit is separately identifiable.

☑ Each job is given a **number** to distinguish it from other jobs.

☑ Costs for each job are collected on a **job cost sheet** or **job card.**

☑ Material costs for each job are determined from **materials requisition notes**.

☑ Labour times on each job are recorded on a **job ticket**, which is then costed and recorded on the job cost sheet.

☑ **Overhead** is absorbed into the cost of jobs using the predetermined overhead absorption rates.

☑ An **internal job costing system** can be used for costing the work of service departments.

☑ **Batch costing** is similar to job costing in that each batch of similar articles is separately identifiable. The **cost per unit** manufactured in a batch is the total batch cost divided by the number of units in the batch.

Quick quiz

1   What is a job?

2   How are the material costs for each job determined?

3   How would you calculate the cost per unit of a completed batch?

Answers to quick quiz

1   A cost unit which consists of a separately identifiable single order or contract.

2   From materials requisition notes, or from suppliers' invoices if materials are purchased specifically for a particular job.

3   $$\frac{\text{Total batch cost}}{\text{Number of units in the batch}}$$

chapter 10

Standard costing

Contents

1 Introduction

We will now turn our attention to **standard costing** and **variance analysis.**

In this chapter we will be looking at the **principles of standard costing** and at how **standard costs can be set** for each of the costs you have studied so far: materials, labour and expenses.

The final chapter will then go on to look at the calculation of variances.

2 Standard costs and standard costing

2.1 What is a standard?

A **standard** represents what we think should happen. It is our best 'guesstimate' of how long something will take to produce, what quantity of materials it will require, how much it will cost and so on.

The **materials standard** for a product is our best estimate of how much material is needed to make the product (standard materials usage) multiplied by our best estimate of the price we will have to pay for the material (standard materials price). For example, we might think that two square metres of material should be needed to make a curtain and that the material should cost £10 per square metre. The standard material cost of the curtain is therefore $2 \times £10 = £20$.

Likewise the **labour standard** for a product is an estimate of how many hours are needed to make the product multiplied by the amount the employee is paid per hour.

2.2 What is standard costing?

Standard costing is the preparation of standard costs for use in the following situations.

- In costing as a means of valuing stocks and the cost of production. It is an alternative method of valuation to methods like LIFO, FIFO or replacement costing.

- In variance analysis, which is a means of controlling the business.

The main use of standard costs is in **variance analysis.** This involves comparing the standard cost with the actual cost to derive a difference, or **variance.** We will look at variance analysis in detail in the next chapter.

2.3 The standard cost card

A **standard cost card** can be prepared for each product or service. The card will normally show the following.

- The **quantity** and **price** of each **direct material** required
- The **time** and **rate** of each **grade of direct labour** required
- The **overhead recovery**
- The **full cost**
- The **standard selling price** and the **standard profit** per unit may also be shown.

A distinction should be made in the standard cost between the following overhead costs.

(a) **Fixed and variable production overheads**, unless variable overheads are insignificant in value, in which case all production overheads are regarded as fixed costs.

(b) **Production overhead and other overheads** (administration and marketing). In many costing systems, administration and marketing overheads are excluded from the standard unit cost, so that the standard cost is simply a standard production cost.

A simple standard cost card might therefore look like this.

STANDARD COST CARD				
PRODUCT 1234				
DESCRIPTION	QUANTITY	COST PER KG/HOUR/ETC	EXTENSION	TOTAL
Materials			£	£
Flour	3 kg	4.00	12.00	
Water	9 litres	2.00	18.00	
SUB-TOTAL				30.00
Labour				
Duckers	6 hrs	10.00	60.00	
Divers	8 hrs	11.00	88.00	
SUB-TOTAL				148.00
Direct cost				178.00
Variable production o/h	14 hrs	0.50		7.00
Standard variable cost				185.00
Fixed production o/h	14 hrs	4.50		63.00
Standard full production cost				248.00
Administration o/h				15.00
STANDARD COST OF SALE				263.00
Standard profit				40.00
STANDARD SELLING PRICE				303.00

In a computer system cost cards could be assembled on a spreadsheet, or by means of a tailor-made programme drawing its information from a database.

2.4 Issue of raw material stock at standard cost

In Chapter 4, we considered the different methods of valuing materials issues and stocks. We briefly mentioned that issues and stock could be valued at a **pre-determined cost,** or what is known as a **standard cost**.

This method is therefore quite simple, since all issues and all closing stock will be valued at the same pre-determined cost.

For example, material A has a standard cost of £8 per unit, it therefore follows that:

(a)   if 200 units of material A are issued, the issues will be valued at 200 × £8 = £1,600;

(b)   if 700 units of material A are held in stock at the year end, the stock valuation of material A will be 700 × £8 = £5,600.

Activity 10.1

(a)   In what senses is a standard cost a 'standard'?
(b)   Why is standard costing used?

3 How standards are set

3.1 Establishing standard material costs

We have already seen that the standard materials cost for a unit of output is calculated as follows.

Standard materials cost = standard materials usage × standard materials price.

To set a standard materials cost we therefore need to establish the **standard materials usage** and the **standard materials price**.

3.2 Standard usage of materials

To ascertain how much material should be used to make a product, technical specifications have to be prepared. This will be done by experts in the production department. On the basis of these technical and engineering specifications and in the light of experience, a **bill of materials** will be drawn up which lists the **quantity of materials** required to make a unit of the product. These quantities can include **allowances for wastage** of materials if that is normal and unavoidable.

3.3 Standard prices of materials

The proper approach to setting a standard price for a particular material is to study the market for that material and become aware of any likely future trends. If your company makes apple pies, news of a disastrous apple crop failure clearly has implications for forecasting raw materials prices.

In practice it is not always possible or practicable to acquire full information. In such circumstances it is likely that **standard prices** would be set on the basis of **current prices** and any notification from suppliers of changes (for example a new catalogue or price list).

Sometimes businesses are able to enter into a contract stating that an agreed price will be charged for an agreed period. Obviously this reduces the uncertainty in the standard setting process.

Standards should also take into account any **discount** that may be available for bulk purchase. Management will need to consider whether it is economical to buy in sufficiently large quantities to earn the discounts, after considering the costs of holding the stock.

3.4 Establishing standard labour costs

In principle it is easy to set **standards for labour**.

(a)   Find out how long it should take to produce a unit.

(b)   Multiply this time by the rate that the person who produces the unit is paid.

Standard labour cost = time it should take to produce a unit × standard labour rate.

In practice, of course, it is not this straightforward. For example, an experienced worker may be able to do the job in less time than a novice, and two equally experienced workers may take a different length of time to do the same job. Some time must be spent **recording actual performance** before a realistic standard can be established.

Example: Labour standards

Fix-a-car Ltd employs two female mechanics, Georgina, who is an apprentice, and Clarissa, who has given loyal service for ten years. The accountant is looking through last week's figures and decides to note down the time each mechanic took to perform each of ten MOT tests.

Georgina	*Clarissa*
Minutes	Minutes
63	30
55	28
50	35
57	25
49	32
52	33
58	29
57	31
70	30
69	27

Georgina is presently paid £4.50 per hour and Clarissa £8 per hour. Calculate the standard time for performing an MOT test and the standard labour cost for performing an MOT test.

Solution

The total time taken for 20 MOT tests is 880 minutes, an average of 44 minutes per test. Georgina takes a total of 580 minutes and Clarissa 300 minutes. Multiplied by their respective hourly rates the total cost is £83.50 or an average of £4.18 per MOT.

We have therefore calculated the following for MOT tests.

Standard time	44 minutes
Standard labour cost per MOT test	£4.18

These figures have considerable shortcomings however.

(a)   They take no account of the time of day when the work was performed, or the type or age of vehicle concerned.

(b)   We cannot tell to what extent the difference in performance of the two mechanics is due to their relative experience and to what extent it is due to other factors: possibly Georgina does the more difficult jobs to gain experience, while Clarissa works on cars that she regularly maintains for established customers who ask for her.

On the other hand it is quite likely that a better controlled set of measurements would give very similar results to those obtained using historical figures. In a case like this there is probably very little point in trying to be more scientific and 'accurate'. Even if the garage performed 20 MOTs a day, the first set of figures would have to be quite significantly wrong for a more accurate estimation to make any significant difference to the accuracy of the costing.

If, however, we were dealing with a high volume business where, say, 10,000 units were produced an hour, then small differences in times and costs per unit (or batch or whatever) would have a considerable impact on the accuracy of the costing. In such cases, the taking of more precise measurements in controlled conditions and the use of **sophisticated statistical techniques** would be worthwhile.

How would these figures affect Georgina and Clarissa if they were used as standards? So far as Georgina is concerned a standard time of 44 minutes is a good target to aim at as she is expected to improve her performance, but she is not expected to be as fast as the more experienced mechanic Clarissa. For Clarissa the standard could be demotivating as she may not work so hard if she knows she has half as long again as she needs to do an MOT.

A 'time saved bonus' for MOT tests taking less than 44 minutes is a good idea in this case: Clarissa will not slack off if she is financially rewarded for her hard work, and Georgina has a further incentive to speed up her own work.

3.5 Work study and standard costs

The point about accuracy might be developed here. In the example no special effort was made to record the times taken to perform the MOT tests. The standard was calculated using **historical data**.

This approach is widely used in practice. It has two **advantages**.

(a)   There is **no extra expense** in obtaining the information.

(b)   The information is not distorted by employees who, knowing they are being measured, **work more slowly than usual** to ensure that easy standards are set.

The information is, however, **distorted by past inefficiencies** and **'engineered standards'** are therefore considered to be preferable. These are based upon a detailed study of the operations involved in a task. You may have heard of **'time and motion studies'**, and this is essentially what is involved although the phrase is rather dated. The most commonly used techniques are the following.

(a)   **Analytical estimating**. This involves breaking down a job into fairly 'large' units and estimating a time for each unit.

(b) **Predetermined motion time study (PMTS).** This approach uses times established for basic human motions and so the physical motions required to perform the task would first need to be ascertained by observation.

(c) **Synthetic timing**. This technique is used if it is not possible to actually measure how long a job takes, perhaps because the job is still at the drawing board stage.

The standard times established by such methods are adjusted to allow for any delays that are unavoidable, and also include an allowance for rest, relaxation, and other contingencies such as machine breakdowns.

Activity 10.2

After extensive work study Carter Ltd has established that all of its production processes are carried out by means of combinations from a set of 10 basic labour operations. A standard time for each operation has been calculated by taking the mean of all observations.

Operation	Time (hours)
1	1 ½
2	1
3	¼
4	2
5	½
6	2
7	3
8	1
9	¼
10	½

Operations 2, 6 and 10 can only be done by trade Y workers and operations 4 and 7 only by grade Z workers.

Grade	Basic wage (per hour)
X	£4.80
Y	£5.50
Z	£6.50

The company now wishes to establish standard direct labour costs for each of its seven major products and its two enhanced packages. The operations involved for each product are as follows.

Product	Operations per unit
A	2, 4, 5
B	2, 5, 6, 10
C	3, 6, 8, 9
Sharp C	1, 3, 4, 6
D	1, 2, 6, 7, 10
E	3, 4, 5, 10
F	1, 4, 9
F (augmented)	3, 6, 7, 8
G	1, 5, 9, 10

Task

Calculate the standard direct labour cost of one unit of each of the nine products.

3.6 Standard hour

A **standard hour** is the amount of work achievable, at standard performance, in an hour.

A standard hour can be a useful measure in standard costing. It is particularly useful when trying to monitor output of a quantity of dissimilar items.

Example: Calculating standard hours of output

T Ltd makes two hand-made products: toy dolls and toy cars. The standard time allowances for the products and the output achieved in the latest two periods are as follows.

	Dolls	Cars
Standard time in hours per unit	2.5	1.0
Output in units:		
period 4	270	120
period 5	130	300

Solution

The products are obviously dissimilar, so it is not very meaningful to simply add together dolls and cars to obtain a figure for total output in each period.

The standard hours produced are calculated as follows.

		Dolls Std. hour		Cars Std. hour	Total Std. hour
Period 4	(270 × 2.5)	675	(120 × 1.0)	120	795
Period 5	(130 × 2.5)	325	(300 × 1.0)	300	625

Thus, although the total number of units produced in period 5 was greater, in terms of **standard hours produced** the actual output was considerably lower than in period 4.

Activity 10.3

FF Ltd operates a fast food restaurant, preparing burger meals and chicken meals.

- The standard time to prepare a burger meal is 10 minutes

- The standard time to prepare a chicken meal is 15 minutes

The output for the last period was as follows.

- 2,400 burger meals prepared
- 1,300 chicken meals prepared

How many standard hours of output were achieved last period?

3.7 Establishing standard costs for expenses

Standard costs for some types of expense can be set with reasonable certainty. Others suffer from the same problems as material and labour.

(a)   If a **contract** has been entered into (for cleaning, say) then the standard cost can be set at the amount specified in the contract.

(b)   Certain expenses are like materials in that there is a **fluctuating market rate** for a specific quantity and the amount likely to be consumed can be determined by 'engineering' methods (studying the relationship between what is put in and what comes out). Examples are gas and electricity.

An advantage (for standard setting purposes) with many expenses is that they are **fixed over the period for which the standard is being set.** The annual buildings insurance premium, for example, will be known for certain at the beginning of the year. It will not turn out to have been different when the year's actual results are determined.

In other cases expenses can be made to conform to a standard. **Discretionary costs,** for example, **need only be incurred up to a certain level.** Suppose you had £10,000 to spend on staff training. Once £10,000 had been spent this would be the end of staff training for the year.

3.8 Standards and inflation

One point to bear in mind is that inflation should be considered when standards are being set. For example, when establishing standard material costs, it is unlikely that the **standard materials usage** of a unit of product will change from one year to the next. The only changes in usage that would arise would be due to fundamental changes in working practices. It is however, likely that the **standard materials price** will increase in line with **inflation**.

Similarly, when establishing standard labour costs, in general, the time it should take to do a job is unlikely to change from year to year. The **standard labour rate** is, however, likely to increase in line with **inflation**.

When revising standards therefore, it is important to take into account how inflation might have an effect on materials prices, labour rates and expenses.

3.9 Recording variances

Earlier in this chapter we mentioned that a major objective of a standard costing system is to **control** an organisation's costs and revenues.

The identification, analysis and reporting of **variances** enables managers to monitor whether standard performance is being achieved. The following types of question can be answered by a detailed analysis of variances.

- Are material prices higher or lower than in the standard cost?
- Is material wastage being kept at standard levels?
- Has it been necessary to pay higher wage rates than expected?

In addition to helping to monitor and control current operations, variance analysis can play a part in **setting standard costs for the future.**

Management may be able to identify persistent variances which are **uncontrollable.** This means that they cannot be corrected by management action. Other favourable variances, where costs are lower than standard, may arise each period and management may attempt to perpetuate them. Examples of persistent variances include the following.

- The electricity supply company has increased unit prices for electricity
- New working practices mean that fewer labour hours are required per unit

This type of variance is likely to continue for the foreseeable future and it can provide valuable information for **updating the standard cost.** The variance will help to signal the extent to which the standard requires alteration. A particular cost may not be causing any significant variances, and there may be no changes foreseen in terms of prices or operations. In this situation it may not be necessary to alter the standard cost for the forthcoming period.

Standards are usually updated once a year. However, a particular standard cost may be no longer achievable and may not represent a **realistic target for control purposes.** When this happens the standard might be updated on an **interim basis** part way through the year, so that it continues to represent a realistic yardstick for planning and control purposes.

4 Performance standards

Do not forget that **standards are averages**. Even under ideal working conditions, it would be unrealistic to expect every unit of activity or production to take exactly the same time, using exactly the same amount of materials, and at exactly the same price. Some variations are inevitable, but for a reasonably large volume of activity, it would be fair to expect that on average, standard results should be achieved.

When we are assessing the **level of performance** expected in a standard, there are four different types of **performance standard** that an organisation could aim for.

- **Ideal standards** are based on the most favourable operating conditions, with no wastage, no inefficiencies, no idle time and no breakdowns. Variances from ideal standards are useful for pinpointing areas where a close examination may result in large savings, but they are likely to have an unfavourable motivational impact. Employees will often feel that the goals are unattainable and not work so hard.

- **Attainable standards** are based on efficient (but not perfect) operating conditions. Some allowance is made for wastage, inefficiencies, machine breakdowns and fatigue. If well-set they provide a useful psychological incentive, and for this reason they should be introduced whenever possible. The consent and co-operation of employees involved in improving the standard are required.

- **Current standards** are standards based on current working conditions (current wastage, current inefficiencies). The disadvantage of current standards is that they do not attempt to improve on current levels of efficiency, which may be poor and capable of significant improvement.

- **Basic standards** are standards which are kept unaltered over a long period of time, and may be out-of-date. They are used to show changes in efficiency or performance over an extended time period. Basic standards are perhaps the least useful and least common type of standard in use.

Activity 10.4

Kingston Ltd makes one product, the tudor. Two types of labour are involved in the preparation of a tudor, skilled and semi-skilled. Skilled labour is paid £10 per hour and semi-skilled £5 per hour. Twice as many skilled labour hours as semi-skilled labour hours are needed to produce a tudor, four semi-skilled labour hours being needed.

A tudor is made up of three different direct materials. Seven kilograms of direct material A, four litres of direct material B and three metres of direct material C are needed. Direct material A costs £1 pe kilogram, direct material B £2 per litre and direct material C £3 per metre.

Variable production overheads are incurred at Kings on Ltd at the rate of £2.50 per direct labour (skilled) hour.

A system of absorption costing is in operation at Kingston Ltd. The basis of absorption is direct labour (skilled) hours. For the forthcoming accounting period, budgeted fixed production overheads are £250,000 and budgeted production of the tudor is 5,000 units.

Task

Using the above information to draw up a standard cost card for the tudor.

Activity 10.5

LW Ltd makes and sells a single product, G, with the following standard specification for materials.

	Quantity	Price per kilogram
	Kilograms	£
Direct material L	10	30
Direct material W	6	45

It takes 30 direct labour hours to produce one unit of G with a standard direct labour cost of £5.50 per hour.

The annual sales/production budget is 1,200 units evenly spread throughout the year.

The annual budgeted production overhead, all fixed, is £252,000 and expenditure is expected to occur evenly over the year, which the company divides into twelve calendar months. Absorption is based on units produced.

The budgeted sales quantity in one particular month was actually sold for a total of £120,000 at the standard selling price.

Task

Calculate the standard product cost and the gross profit of each unit sold.

Activity 10.6

The following times were recorded for the performance of a task in the last month.

Worker	Time	Time
Lynn	1 hour 45 minutes	2 hours
Alison	2 hours 5 minutes	1 hour 55 minutes
Jed	1 hour 15 minutes	1 hour 15 minutes
Kate	2 hours 10 minutes	1 hour 30 minutes
Nick	1 hour 45 minutes	1 hour 37 minutes
Edmund	1 hour 39 minutes	1 hour 57 minutes
Bob	2 hours	1 hour 30 minutes
Roger	2 hours 15 minutes	1 hour 43 minutes
Tina	1 hour 20 minutes	1 hour 35 minutes
Tim	2 hours 20 minutes	2 hours 2 minutes
Clive	1 hour 35 minutes	1 hours 52 minutes
Graham	1 hour 59 minutes	2 hours 5 minutes
Barry	1 hour 40 minutes	2 hours
Glen	1 hour 57 minutes	1 hour 53 minutes

The standard time for the performance of the task is 2 hours and 30 minutes, but this was set several years ago when most staff were unfamiliar with the equipment in use. It is estimated that at least 15 minutes of idle time may be unavoidable.

Task

Determine four performance standards for the task in question.

Activity 10.7

The following information has been collected about the materials used by Sutton Ltd, an organisation which uses standard costing.

Material	Supplier	Information source	Unit cost £	20X2 standard £	20X3 standard £
AB30	4073	20X3 catalogue	1.74	1.68	
AB35	4524	20X2 catalogue	5.93	5.93	
		Invoice (10/X2)	6.05		
		Telephone enquiry to 4524	6.00		
BB29	4333	X2/X3 catalogue	15.72	15.00	
BB42	4929	Invoice (5/X2)	2.36	2.40	
	-	New supplier quotation (11/X2)	1.94		
CA19	4124	Contract to 12/X3	20.07	20.07	
		Invoice (12/X2)	21.50		
CD26	4828	-		2.50	

Sutton Ltd uses the materials in a variety of combinations to make four different products. Technical specifications for usage (in units of material per batch) have been determined as follows.

Material	Guildford	Dorking	Reigate	Coulsdon
AB30	20	20	10	5
AB35	-	10	-	-
BB29	-	-	4	-
BB42	8	5	-	12
CA19	20	9	-	5
CD26	6	-	3	-

Tasks

(a) What are the 20X2 standard materials costs for each product?

(b) As a last resort standard costs are set by adding the current annual rate of inflation to the most recent available price, but more certain information is used if it is available (for example, catalogue prices are usually guaranteed for 12 months). Your task is to calculate the new standard costs for 20X3. Very large quantities are used so it is important to calculate to the nearest penny. The RPI is 3.7%.

Key learning points

- ☑ A **standard** represents what we think should happen.

- ☑ A **standard cost** is a predetermined unit of cost.

- ☑ **Standard costing** is a means of valuing stocks and the issue of materials to production and a way of exercising control over a business.

- ☑ A **standard cost card** shows full details of the standard cost of a product.

- ☑ Setting **materials standards** involves determining how much material is needed to produce a product and the price of that material.

- ☑ Setting standard **labour times** is generally a matter of estimating how long it will take to do a piece of work. This can be done on a rough and ready basis or by detailed work study.

- ☑ **Standard costs** can be set for expenses just as they can for any other cost.

- ☑ Standards are basically set by developing an awareness of market conditions and by understanding technical requirements.

- ☑ Standards can also be set so as to encourage improvements in performance.

- ☑ **Inflation** should always be considered when setting standards.

Quick quiz

1   What details would you expect to see on a standard cost card?

2   What is the formula for standard materials cost?

3   What is the formula for standard labour cost?

4   What are the advantages of using historical data to calculate labour standards?

5   How would you explain the term standard hour?

6   List four types of performance standard.

7   How often are standard cost revisions usually made?

Answers to quick quiz

1   The quantity and price of direct material. The time and rate of each grade of direct labour. Overhead recovery, full cost, standard selling price and standard profit.

2   Standard materials usage × standard materials price.

3   Time that it should take to produce a unit × standard labour rate per hour.

4   No extra costs are involved in getting the information, and the information is not distorted by employees working more quickly or slowly than usual.

5   The quantity of work that could be produced in one hour, working at the standard rate of performance.

6   Ideal, attainable, current and basic.

7   Once a year.

chapter 11

Calculation of
variances

Contents

1 Introduction

Having set **standards** (as described in the previous chapter), what are we going to do with them? We mentioned that we could use materials standards to value materials issues and materials stock. But what about labour standards? And standards for expenses? **The principal reason most organisations use standard costs is for control.**

In the previous chapter we introduced you to the term 'variance'. When costs are incurred they are compared with the estimated standard cost, and if there is a difference it is known as a **variance**. Generally, somebody will be responsible for a variance and will be asked to explain why it occurred.

The analysis of variances is a very important aspect of costing. Variance analysis simply aims to find the difference between what costs **were** and what they **should have been**. In this chapter you will be learning how the analysis is done.

2 Variances

Standards represent what should happen. Suppose for example that 10,000 units of product X should require 10,000 kg of material A costing £10,000. This is therefore the standard for product X. Let us now consider the actual results for product X – 11,000 kg of material A costing £12,000 were required to make 10,000 units of product X. We can therefore deduce the following.

(a) We had to spend £2,000 more on materials than we should have to make 10,000 units of product X.

(b) We used 1,000 kg more of material A than we should have to make 10,000 units of product X.

These differences that we have identified are the **variances** that we were explaining above.

- A **variance** is the difference between an actual result and an expected standard cost or revenue.

- **Variance analysis** is the process by which the *total* difference between standard and actual results is analysed.

Variances may be either **favourable** or **adverse**.

- A **favourable** variance means that actual results were better than standard
- An **adverse** variance means that actual results were worse than standard

3 Materials variances

3.1 Why materials variances arise

Standards are estimates: they are predictions of what will happen. However, the accuracy of these estimates will depend upon what happens after they have been set.

For example, suppose you are expecting a good coffee bean harvest, and therefore set a **standard material price** of £10 per kg of coffee. If your prediction is correct, and a good harvest results, then your standard of £10 will be correct. However, if your prediction is not correct, and prices are in fact £15 per kg of coffee beans, then **your standard will be inaccurate.**

If your standard is inaccurate, then the actual costs incurred will be different to the standard costs estimated − and this is where our **differences** or **variances** arise.

Think back to how the **materials standard cost** is calculated.

materials standard cost = standard usage × standard price

Now think about how a variance could arise. Consider the following.

- If actual usage were different to standard usage
- If actual price were different to standard price
- If actual usage **and** actual price were **both** different to standard

3.2 Calculating materials variances

Example: Materials variances

The following standards have been set for product LW.

	Standard price	Standard usage
Material A	£2.20 per kg	2kg per unit

In February, the actual production and material usage figures were as follows.

Actual production	10,000 units
Material A	21,000 kg costing £47,250

Task

Calculate the following variances for February.

(a) Material total variance
(b) Material price variance
(c) Material usage variance

Solution

(a) **The material total variance**

	£
10,000 units of product LW should have cost (× £2.20 × 2kg)	44,000
but did cost	47,250
Material total variance	3,250 (A)

The (A) denotes an **adverse** variance. The variance is adverse because the units cost more than they should have cost.

Now we can analyse the material total variance into its two constituent parts: the **material price variance** and the **material usage variance**.

(b)   **The material price variance**

This is the difference between the price that should have been paid for 21,000 kg, and the price that was paid.

	£
21,000 kg should have cost (× £2.20)	46,200
but did cost	47,250
Material price variance	1,050 (A)

The price variance is adverse because the price paid for the material was higher than standard.

(c)   **The material usage variance**

This is the difference between how many kilograms of material A should have been used to produce 10,000 units of product LW and how many kilograms were used, valued at the standard price per kilogram.

10,000 units should have used (× 2 kg)	20,000 kg
but did use	21,000 kg
Material usage variance in kg	1,000 kg
× standard price per kg	× £2.20
Material usage variance	£2,200 (A)

The usage variance is adverse because more material was used than should have been used.

- The **material total variance** is the difference between what the output actually cost and what it should have cost, in terms of material. It can be divided into the following two sub-variances.

- The **material price variance** is the difference between the standard price and the actual price of the *actual* quantity of material used or purchased. In other words, it is the difference between what the material did cost and what it should have cost.

- The **material usage variance** is the difference between the standard quantity of materials that *should* have been used for the number of units *actually* produced, and the actual quantity of materials used, valued at the standard price per unit of material. In other words, it is the difference between how much material should have been used and how much material was used, valued at standard cost.

The variances can be **summarised** as follows.

	£
Material price variance	1,050 (A)
Material usage variance	2,200 (A)
Material total variance	3,250 (A)

3.3 Adverse and favourable variances

All of the examples we have seen so far have been cases where **more money was paid out** or **more materials were used than expected**. These are called **adverse variances** because they have adverse consequences. They mean that **less profit** is made than we hoped.

Sometimes, of course, things will be cheaper than usual or we will use them more efficiently. When less money is paid than expected or fewer materials are used than expected the variances are said to be **favourable variances**. They mean that **more profit** is made than we hoped.

Example: Adverse and favourable variances

It is now April and actual data for product LW is as follows.

Production	9,500 units
Material A	20,000 kg costing £42,000

Have a go at calculating the variances yourself before looking at the solution.

Solution

(a) Let's begin by calculating the **material total variance**.

	£
9,500 units should have cost (9,500 × 2kg × £2.20)	41,800
but did cost	42,000
Material total variance	200 (A)

The (A) indicates that overall the variance is **adverse**.

(b) We can now go on to calculate the individual components of the total variance (ie the price and usage variances).

	£
20,000 kg should have cost (× £2.20)	44,000
but did cost	42,000
Material price variance	2,000 (F)

The (F) indicates that this is a **favourable** variance because less money was spent than expected.

9,500 units should use (× 2 kg)	19,000 kg
but did use	20,000 kg
Material usage variance in kg	1,000 kg (A)
× standard price per kg	× £2.20
Material usage variance in £	£2,200 (A)

The (A) indicates that this is an **adverse** variance, because more materials were used than standard for 9,500 units.

(c)   Let's check that the total variance is the sum of the two individual variances.

	£
Price variance	2,000 (F)
Usage variance	(2,200) (A)
Total variance	(200) (A)

Remember that adverse variances are **negative** (*less* profit) and favourable variances are **positive** (*more* profit).

3.4 Material variances and opening and closing stock

Suppose that a company uses raw material P in production, and that this raw material has a standard price of £3 per metre. During one month 6,000 metres are bought for £18,600, and 5,000 metres are used in production. At the end of the month, stock will have been increased by 1,000 metres. In variance analysis, the problem is to determine the material price variance. Should it be calculated on the basis of **materials purchased** (6,000 metres) or on the basis of **materials used** (5,000 metres)?

The answer to this problem depends on how **closing stocks** of the raw materials will be valued.

(a)   If they are **valued at standard price**, (1,000 units at £3 per unit) the **price variance is calculated on material purchases** in the period.

(b)   If they are **valued at actual cost** (FIFO) (1,000 units at £3.10 per unit) the **price variance is calculated on materials used in production** in the period.

A **full standard costing system** is usually in operation and therefore the price variance is usually calculated on **purchases** in the period. We will return to consider this aspect of variance analysis in more detail in the next chapter.

Activity 11.1

Calculate the material total variance and its sub-variances given the following information.

Product A has a standard direct materials cost of £10 (5 kg of material M). During April 100 units of product A were manufactured using 520 kg of material M at a cost of £1,025.

4 Labour variances

Labour variances are very similar to materials variances but they have different names. There are two types of sub-variance that you need to understand and calculate for labour. The 'money' variance is called the **rate variance** and the 'quantity' variance is called the **efficiency variance**.

- The **labour total variance** is the difference between what the output should have cost and what it did cost, in terms of labour. It can be divided into the following two sub-variances.

- The **labour rate variance** is the difference between the standard rate and the actual rate for the actual number of hours paid for. In other words, it is the difference between what the labour did cost and what it should have cost.

- The **labour efficiency variance** is the difference between the hours that *should* have been worked for the number of units *actually* produced, and the actual number of hours worked, valued at the standard rate per hour. In other words, it is the difference between how many hours should have been worked and how many hours were worked, valued at the standard rate per hour.

Example: Labour variances

Suppose that the labour standard for the production of a unit of product B is as follows.

> 2 hours of grade S labour at £6 per hour = £12 per unit

During May 200 units of product B were made and the direct labour cost of grade S labour was £2,418 for 390 hours work.

Task

Calculate the following variances.

(a)   The direct labour total variance
(b)   The direct labour rate variance
(c)   The direct labour efficiency variance

Solution

(a)   Let us begin by calculating the **direct labour total variance**.

	£
200 units of product B should have cost (× £12)	2,400
but did cost	2,418
Direct labour total variance	18 (A)

Having learned that direct labour costs were £18 more than they should have been, we can now look at why this happened.

(b)   **Labour rate variance**. This variance is calculated by taking the number of labour hours 'purchased' ie paid for, and comparing what they did cost with what they should have cost.

	£
390 hours of grade S labour should cost (× £6)	2,340
but did cost	2,418
Labour rate variance	78 (A)

The variance is **adverse** because **actual rates of pay were higher than expected.**

(c)   **Labour efficiency variance**. This variance is calculated by taking the amount of output produced (200 units of product B) and comparing how long it should have taken to produce them with how long it did take. The difference is the **efficiency variance**, expressed in hours of work. It should be converted into £ by applying the **standard rate per labour hour**.

200 units of product B should take (× 2 hours)	400 hrs
but did take	390 hrs
Labour efficiency variance in hrs	10 hrs (F)
× standard rate per hour	× £6
Labour efficiency variance in £	£60 (F)

The variance is **favourable** because the **labour force has been more efficient** than expected.

(d)   **Summary**

	£
Labour rate variance	78 (A)
Labour efficiency variance	60 (F)
Direct labour total variance	18 (A)

Activity 11.2

Pogle Ltd manufactures one product, the clanger. The following direct standard costs apply to the clanger.

	£
Direct material 10 kgs at £5 per kg	50
Direct labour 5 hours at £6 per hour	30

In July production was 10,000 units and actual data for the month was:

(a)   Actual materials consumed 106,000 kgs costing £530,500

(b)   Actual labour hours worked 50,200 hours, costing £307,200

Task

Calculate the material price and usage variances, and the labour rate and efficiency variances.

5 Fixed overhead variances

You may have noticed that the method of calculating cost variances for variable cost items is essentially the same for labour and materials. Fixed overhead variances are very different. In an absorption costing system, they are **an attempt to explain the under– or over-absorption of fixed production overheads in production costs**. You should of course, know all about under/over absorption of fixed overheads. We looked at this topic in detail in Chapter 7. If you need reminding, however, skim through Section 8 of that chapter again.

You will find it easier to calculate and understand **fixed overhead variances**, if you keep in mind the whole time that you are trying to 'explain' (put a name and value to) any under– or over-absorbed overhead.

Remember that the **absorption rate** is calculated as follows.

$$\textbf{Overhead absorption rate } = \frac{\text{Budgeted fixed overhead}}{\text{Budgeted activity level}}$$

If either of the following are incorrect, then we will have an under or over absorption of overhead.

- The numerator (number on top) = budgeted fixed overhead
- The denominator (number on bottom) = budgeted activity level

The **fixed overhead total variance** may be broken down into two parts as follows.

- An **expenditure variance**
- A **volume variance**. This in turn may be split into two parts.

    – An efficiency variance
    – A capacity variance

5.1 The fixed overhead expenditure variance

The fixed overhead expenditure variance occurs if the numerator is incorrect. It measures the under– or over-absorbed overhead caused by the **actual total overhead** being different from the budgeted total overhead.

5.2 The fixed overhead volume variance

As we have already stated, the fixed overhead volume variance is made up of the following sub-variances.

- Fixed overhead efficiency variance
- Fixed overhead capacity variance

The fixed overhead efficiency and capacity variances measure the under– or over-absorbed overhead caused by the **actual activity level** being different from the budgeted activity level used in calculating the absorption rate.

There are two reasons why the **actual activity level** may be different from the **budgeted activity level** used in calculating the absorption rate.

(a) The workforce may have worked more or less efficiently than the standard set. This deviation is measured by the **fixed overhead efficiency variance.**

(b) The hours worked by the workforce could have been different to the original budgeted hours (regardless of the level of efficiency of the workforce) because of overtime and strikes etc. This deviation from the standard is measured by the **fixed overhead capacity variance.**

5.3 How to calculate the variances

In order to clarify the overhead variances which we have encountered in this section, consider the following definitions which are expressed in terms of how each overhead variance should be calculated.

- **Fixed overhead total variance** is the difference between fixed overhead incurred and fixed overhead absorbed. In other words, it is the under– or over-absorbed fixed overhead.

- **Fixed overhead expenditure variance** is the difference between the budgeted fixed overhead expenditure and actual fixed overhead expenditure.

- **Fixed overhead volume variance** is the difference between actual and budgeted production/volume multiplied by the standard absorption rate per **unit** or per **standard hour**.

- **Fixed overhead efficiency variance** is the difference between the number of hours that actual production should have taken, and the number of hours actually taken (that is, worked) multiplied by the standard absorption rate per **hour**.

- **Fixed overhead capacity variance** is the difference between the original budgeted hours of work and the actual hours worked, multiplied by the standard absorption rate per **hour**.

You should now be ready to work through an example to demonstrate all of the fixed overhead variances.

Example: Fixed overhead variances

Suppose that a company budgets to produce 1,000 units of product E during August 20X3. The expected time to produce a unit of E is five hours, and the budgeted fixed overhead is £20,000. The standard fixed overhead cost per unit of product E will therefore be as follows.

$$5 \text{ hours at £4 per hour } = \text{£20 per unit}$$

Actual fixed overhead expenditure in August 20X3 turns out to be £20,450. The labour force manages to produce 1,100 units of product E in 5,400 hours of work.

Task

Calculate the following variances.

(a)   The fixed overhead total variance
(b)   The fixed overhead expenditure variance
(c)   The fixed overhead volume variance
(d)   The fixed overhead efficiency variance
(e)   The fixed overhead capacity variance

Solution

All of the variances assess the under or over absorption of fixed overheads.

(a)   **Fixed overhead total variance**

	£
Fixed overhead incurred	20,450
Fixed overhead absorbed (1,100 units × £20 per unit)	22,000
Fixed overhead total variance	1,550 (F)
(= under-/over-absorbed overhead)	

The variance is favourable because more overheads were absorbed than incurred.

(b) **Fixed overhead expenditure variance**

	£
Budgeted fixed overhead expenditure	20,000
Actual fixed overhead expenditure	20,450
Fixed overhead expenditure variance	450 (A)

The variance is adverse because actual expenditure was greater than budgeted expenditure.

(c) **Fixed overhead volume variance**

The production volume achieved was greater than expected. The fixed overhead volume variance measures the difference at the standard rate.

Actual production volume achieved	1,100 units
Budgeted production volume	1,000 units
Volume variance in units	100 units (F)
× standard absorption rate per unit	× £20
Fixed overhead volume variance	£2,000 (F)

The variance is **favourable** because output was greater than expected.

(i) The labour force may have worked efficiently, and produced output at a faster rate than expected. Since overheads are absorbed at the rate of £20 per unit, more will be absorbed if units are produced more quickly. This **efficiency variance** is exactly the same in hours as the direct labour efficiency variance, but is valued in £ at the standard absorption rate for fixed overhead.

(ii) The labour force may have worked longer hours than budgeted, and therefore produced more output, so there may be a **capacity variance**.

(d) **Fixed overhead efficiency variance**

The efficiency variance is calculated in the same way as the labour efficiency variance.

1,100 units of product E should take (× 5 hrs)	5,500 hrs
but did take	5,400 hrs
Fixed overhead efficiency variance in hours	100 hrs (F)
× standard fixed overhead absorption rate per hour	× £4
Fixed overhead efficiency variance in £	£400 (F)

The labour force has produced 5,500 standard hours of work in 5,400 actual hours. Therefore output is 100 standard hours (or 20 units of product E) higher than budgeted and the variance is **favourable**.

(e) **Fixed overhead capacity variance**

The capacity variance is the difference between the budgeted hours of work and the actual active hours of work.

Budgeted hours of work	5,000 hrs
Actual hours worked	5,400 hrs
Fixed overhead capacity variance in hours	400 hrs (F)
× standard fixed overhead absorption rate per hour	× £4
Fixed overhead capacity variance in £	£1,600 (F)

Since the labour force worked 400 hours longer than budgeted, we should expect output to be 400 standard hours (or 80 units of product E) higher than budgeted. Hence the variance is **favourable**.

The variances may be summarised as follows.

	£
Expenditure variance	450 (A)
Efficiency variance	400 (F)
Capacity variance	1,600 (F)
Over-absorbed overhead (total variance)	£1,550 (F)

Activity 11.3

Constance & Co Ltd expected to produce 14,000 units of its product during September 20X3. The standard time for a unit of the product is 2 hours and the budgeted fixed production overhead was £70,000.

In the event the actual fixed overhead expenditure was £67,500. The number of hours worked was 28,400 and 12,000 units were produced.

Task

Calculate all of the fixed overhead variances for September 20X3.

5.4 Measuring activity in terms of standard hours

In Chapter 10 you learned that activity can be measured in terms of **standard hours.** This is particularly useful if an organisation produces dissimilar products.

When an organisation manufactures dissimilar products, standard hours must be used as the basis for calculating overhead variances. The method of calculation does not alter, as the following example will demonstrate.

Example: Fixed overhead variances based on standard hours

The following information is provided for the machining department last period.

Budgeted overhead	£185,000
Budgeted machine hours	37,000
Actual machine hours	36,000
Standard machine hours produced	36,600
Actual overheads incurred	£205,000

Task

Calculate the fixed overhead variances for the machining department last period.

Solution

Remember that the **method of calculation does not alter:** we simply use 'standard hours of production' in place of 'units of production'.

Fixed overhead absorption rate = $\dfrac{£185,000}{37,000}$ = £5 per standard machine hour

Fixed overhead total variance

	£
	£
Fixed overhead incurred	205,000
Fixed overhead absorbed (36,600 std hours × £5)	183,000
Fixed overhead total variance	22,000 (A)

Fixed overhead expenditure variance

	£
	£
Budgeted fixed overhead expenditure	185,000
Actual fixed overhead expenditure	205,000
Fixed overhead expenditure variance	20,000 (A)

Fixed overhead volume variance

Actual production volume achieved	36,600 std hrs
Budgeted production volume	37,000 std hrs
Volume variance in std. hrs	400 std hrs (A)
× std. absorption rate per std. hour	× £5
Fixed overhead volume variance	£2,000 (A)

Check: Volume £2,000 (A) + Expenditure £20,000 (A) = Total £22,000 (A)

Fixed overhead efficiency variance

Standard time for output achieved	36,600 hours
Actual hours taken	36,000 hours
Fixed overhead efficiency variance in hours	600 hours (F)
× std. absorption rate per hour	× £5
Fixed overhead efficiency variance	£3,000 (F)

Fixed overhead capacity variance

Budgeted hours of work	37,000
Actual hours worked	36,000
Capacity variance in hours	1,000 hours (A)
× std. absorption rate per hour	× £5
Fixed overhead capacity variance	£5,000 (A)

Check: Efficiency £3,000 (F) + Capacity £5,000 (A) = Volume £2,000(A)

Activity 11.4

SH Ltd makes products S and H. Data for the products and for activity last period are as follows.

- Standard time allowances are 10 minutes per unit of product S and 20 minutes per unit of product H
- Budgeted overhead for the period = £4,500
- Actual overhead incurred during period = £5,200
- Budgeted production for period = 4,200 units of S; 2,400 units of H
- Activity achieved during period = 3,600 units of S; 3,000 units of H
- Hours worked during period = 1,800

Task

Calculate the following variances for the period

(a) Fixed overhead expenditure variance
(b) Fixed overhead volume variance
(c) Fixed overhead capacity variance
(d) Fixed overhead efficiency variance

Activity 11.5

Lynn Ltd produces and sells the Koob, the standard cost for one unit being as follows.

	£
Direct material A – 10 kilograms at £20 per kg	200
Direct material B – 5 litres at £6 per litre	30
Direct wages – 5 hours at £6 per hour	30
Fixed overhead	50
Total standard cost	310

The fixed overhead included in the standard cost is based on an expected monthly output of 900 units. Fixed overhead is absorbed on the basis of direct labour hours.

During April 20X3 the actual results were as follows.

Production	800 units
Material A	7,800 kg used, costing £159,900
Material B	4,300 litres used, costing £23,650
Direct wages	4,200 hours worked for £24,150
Fixed overhead	£47,000

Tasks

(a) Calculate price and usage variances for each material.
(b) Calculate labour rate and efficiency variances.
(c) Calculate fixed overhead expenditure, volume, efficiency and capacity variances.

6 Control ratios

6.1 Efficiency, capacity and activity (production volume) ratios

In Chapter 5 you saw how labour activity can be measured by ratios as follows.

- Efficiency ratio
- Capacity ratio
- Activity ratio or production volume ratio

Efficiency ratio

$$\frac{\text{Standard hours to make actual output}}{\text{Actual hours worked}}$$

Capacity ratio

$$\times \frac{\text{Actual hours worked}}{\text{Hours budgeted}}$$

Activity ratio

$$= \frac{\text{Output measured in expected or standard hours}}{\text{Hours budgeted}}$$

These ratios are usually expressed as percentages.

Example: Ratios

Rush and Fluster Ltd budgets to make 25,000 standard units of output (in four hours each) during a budget period of 100,000 hours.

Actual output during the period was 27,000 units which took 120,000 hours to make.

Task

Calculate the efficiency, capacity and activity (production volume) ratios.

Solution

(a) Efficiency ratio $\dfrac{(27,000 \times 4)\text{hours}}{120,000 \text{ hours}} \times 100\% = 90\%$

(b) Capacity ratio $\dfrac{120,000 \text{hours}}{100,000 \text{hours}} \times 100\% = 120\%$

(c) Activity ratio $\dfrac{(27,000 \times 4)\text{hours}}{100,000 \text{ hours}} \times 100\% = 108\%$

(d) The production volume (activity) ratio of 108% (more output than budgeted) is explained by the 120% capacity working, offset to a certain extent by the poor efficiency (90% × 120% = 108%).

The ratios that we have calculated provide equivalent information to the **overhead variances,** but in a **non-monetary** form.

(a)   The **efficiency** ratio is equivalent to the **overhead efficiency variance.** The ratio of **below 100%** would be represented by an **adverse** efficiency variance. It is worth noting that the **labour efficiency variance** would also be adverse.

(b)   The **capacity** ratio is equivalent to the **overhead capacity variance.** The ratio of **above 100%** would be represented by a **favourable** capacity variance.

(c)   The **activity** or **production volume** ratio is equivalent to the **overhead volume variance.** The ratio of **above 100%** would be represented by a **favourable** volume variance.

7 The reasons for cost variances

There are many possible reasons for cost variances arising, as you will see from the following list of possible causes.

(a) Material price	Unforeseen discounts received More care taken in purchasing Change in material standard	Price increase Careless purchasing Change in material standard
(b) Material usage	Material used of higher quality than standard More effective use made of material Errors in allocating material to jobs	Defective material Excessive waste Theft Stricter quality control Errors in allocating material to jobs
(c) Labour rate	Use of apprentices or other workers at a rate of pay lower than standard	Wage rate increase Use of higher grade labour
(d) Labour Efficiency	Output produced more quickly than expected because of work motivation, better quality of equipment or materials, or better methods Errors in allocating time to jobs	Lost time in excess of standard allowed Output lower than standard set because of deliberate restriction, lack of training, or sub-standard material used Errors in allocating time to jobs
(e) Overhead expenditure	Savings in costs incurred More economical use of services	Increase in cost of services used Excessive use of services Change in type of services used
(f) Overhead capacity	Extra overtime was worked More employees taken on	Machine breakdowns Shortage of materials
(g) Overhead efficiency	As for labour efficiency	As for labour efficiency

Once variances have been calculated, management have to decide whether or not to investigate their causes. It would be extremely **time consuming and expensive** to investigate every variance therefore managers have to decide which variances are significant.

A number of factors can be taken into account when deciding whether a variance is significant.

(a) **Materiality.** A standard cost is really only an **average** expected cost and is not a rigid specification. Small variations either side of this average are therefore bound to occur. The problem is to decide whether a variation from standard should be considered **significant** and worthy of investigation. **Tolerance limits** can be set and only variances which exceed such limits would require investigating.

(b) **Controllability.** Some types of variance may not be controllable even once their cause is discovered. For example, if there is a general worldwide increase in the price of a raw material there is nothing that can be done internally to control the effect of this.

(c) **The type of standard being used.**

  (i) The efficiency variance reported in any control period, whether for materials or labour, will depend on the **efficiency level** set. If, for example, an **ideal standard** is used, variances will always be **adverse**.

  (ii) A similar problem arises if **average price levels** are used as standards. If inflation exists, favourable price variances are likely to be reported at the beginning of a period, to be offset by adverse price variances later in the period as inflation pushes prices up.

(d) **Interdependence between variances**. Quite possibly, individual variances should not be looked at in isolation. One variance might be inter-related with another, and much of it might have occurred only because the other, inter-related, variance occurred too.

7.1 Interdependence between variances

When two variances are interdependent (interrelated) one will usually be adverse and the other one favourable. Here are some examples.

7.1.1 Materials price and usage

It may be decided to purchase cheaper materials for a job in order to obtain a **favourable price variance**. This may result in higher materials wastage and an **adverse usage variance**. If the cheaper materials are more difficult to handle, there might also be some **adverse labour efficiency** variance.

7.1.2 Labour rate and efficiency

If employees are paid higher rates for experience and skill, using a highly skilled team to do some work would incur an **adverse rate variance**, but should also obtain a **favourable efficiency variance**. In contrast, a **favourable rate variance** might indicate a larger-than-expected proportion of inexperienced workers in the workforce. This could result in an **adverse labour efficiency variance,** and perhaps poor materials handling and high rates of rejects too (**adverse materials usage variance**).

Activity 11.6

(a) Give two possible reasons for an adverse material price variance.
(b) What variances might arise if temporary student labour is used on a job?

Key learning points

☑ A **variance** is the difference between actual results and standard results. **Variance analysis** is the process by which the total difference between actual results and standard results is analysed.

☑ In general, a **favourable** variance arises when actual results are better than standard results, an **adverse** variance means that actual results were worse than standard.

☑ **Total**, **price** and **usage** variances may be calculated for materials.

☑ **Total**, **rate** and **efficiency** variances may be calculated for labour.

☑ **Fixed overhead variances** include the following.

– **Expenditure** variance

– **Volume** variance (which may be split into **efficiency** and **capacity**)

☑ When an organisation manufactures **dissimilar units**, **standard hours** must be used as the basis for calculating overhead variances.

☑ When considering the reasons why variances have occurred, it is important to remember that they should not be looked at in isolation, since there may be **interdependence between variances**.

Quick quiz

1   What is a material usage variance?

2   What do favourable variances mean in terms of profit?

3   List three possible reasons why an adverse material usage variance might occur.

4   The fixed overhead volume variance is broken down into which two sub-variances?

5   What is the fixed overhead total variance and what is it equivalent to?

6   Which of the following formulae is correct?

   (a)   Efficiency ratio × capacity ratio = activity ratio
   (b)   Efficiency ratio × activity ratio = capacity ratio
   (c)   Capacity ratio × activity ratio = efficiency ratio

Answers to quick quiz

1   The difference between the standard quantity of materials that should have been used for the number of units actually produced, and the actual quantity of materials used, valued at the standard price per unit of material.

2   They mean the actual profits are higher than standard profits.

3   •   Material is defective
   •   There is an excessive waste of material
   •   Theft
   •   Stricter quality control

4   The overhead efficiency variance and the overhead capacity variance.

5   It is the difference between fixed overhead incurred and fixed overhead absorbed. It is equivalent to the under– or over-absorbed overhead.

6   (a)   Efficiency ratio × capacity ratio = activity ratio

Answers to
Activities

Chapter 1

Answer 1.1

Tutorial note. In (a) the information is not precise enough, in (b) you are not comparing like with like and in (c) other comparisons are needed.

(a) Daily figures will not help the supervisor to judge the performance of his particular shift (there are other shifts during the day).

(b) You would expect December sales to be the highest for the year so comparison with December last year and the year-to-date with last year might be more meaningful.

(c) Exam results only measure one aspect of a school's objectives and will be affected by the quality of pupils as well as teachers.

Answer 1.2

Tutorial note. In (b) you need to quantify why the differences arose.

(a) Actual sales revenue could be found in the ledger accounts for sales.

(b)

Sales Revenue Report April to June

April		May		June		Total	
Actual	Budgeted	Actual	Budgeted	Actual	Budgeted	Actual	Budgeted
£'000	£'000	£'000	£'000	£'000	£'000	£'000	£'000
9.0	8.8	10.2	9.6	11.8	11.9	31.0	30.3

Note

Sales revenue for the three months is £700 more than budgeted.

In April, the quantity sold was greater than budget resulting in £200 revenue over budget. In May, a price rise of 50p per gallon (not in the budget until June) resulted in an increase in revenue of £600 over budget although the amount sold was as planned. In June, the quantity sold was under budget resulting in a £100 revenue shortfall.

Answer 1.3

Tutorial note. The key to this activity is determining who makes the decisions about which costs.

(a) Nursing salaries would probably be centrally controlled by the hospital and influenced by NHS salaries. Drugs would be determined by a doctor and administered by a nurse. Dressings are probably the only item the ward sister has any control over.

(b) The £300 drugs cost for March looks quite different from the normal pattern of cost. You should look at the ledger account and purchase documents to see if it is correct.

(c)   Combining drugs and dressings costs does not seem helpful in a ward report since only one is likely to be a controllable cost for the ward sister.

Answer 1.4

Tutorial note. Using % increase may result in small £ changes being highlighted (if budgeted cost is £1, actual cost is £3, the variance is 200%). However % variances may be a good guide to problems with the assumptions behind budgets.

(a)

	Budgeted £	Actual £	Variance £	Variance %
Laundry	1,000	1,045	45(A)	4.5
Heat and light	1,500	1,420	80(F)	5.3
Catering	8,500	8,895	395(A)	4.6
Nursing staff	7,000	6,400	600(F)	8.6
Ancillary staff	10,600	10,950	350(A)	3.3

$$\text{Variance \%} = \frac{\text{Actual costs} - \text{Budgeted costs}}{\text{Budgeted costs}} \times 100\%$$

(b)   Only the cost of nursing staff

(c)   Heat and light and nursing staff

Answer 1.5

Tutorial note. This illustrates not only the importance of non-financial objectives, but also how failure to meet non-financial objectives may impact upon financial objectives.

This is only good if the necessary standards of cleanliness can be maintained. If they can be, then there were probably too many cleaners before. If standards fall, there will be other effects (like more patient infections) which will cost more in the long term and damage the chief goal of improving health.

Answer 1.6

Tutorial note. Note that the action to control the variance may be needed by Brown or the manager.

(a)

Variances	Month 4	YTD
Green	£500 (favourable)	£5,000 (favourable)
Brown	£400 (adverse)	£5,000 (adverse)

(b)   The variances may be controllable. The manager needs to find out why Brown is below target. If he has been sick or on holiday, he may need to make more calls in the next few months. However, he may need more training or greater incentives; if so the manager should try to provide what he needs.

(c)   The action taken depends on the reasons for both variances. Total sales for the regions are as planned for the year so far, so there is no effect on the production plan. The manager should assess whether Brown is really underperforming (see part (b)). Alternatively Brown may have more 'difficult' customers than Green. If so, the manager should consider changing targets or swapping some customers between the two salesmen.

Answer 1.7

Tutorial note. Another illustration of the importance of non-financial objectives.

(a)   The suggestions miss the point that the library does not seem to be meeting the needs of staff and students. Until this is remedied, there is no point (and probably no chance) of taking over staff stocks. Using information staff for cataloguing is not likely to improve library service either.

(b)   Library performance cannot be measured only in terms of money since low spending might mean that staff books, facilities etc are insufficient rather than that it is efficiently run.

(c)   Other measures should reflect the goals of the library service. These could include levels of usage (perhaps analysed by department), surveys of customer satisfaction, new books purchased, numbers of enquiries dealt with etc.

Answer 1.8

Tutorial note. In answering activities such as (a), you need to think about how what one department does can affect another. In (b) quantities sold might also be important as well as sales revenue. A decrease in quantity may imply that the business's share of the market has decreased.

(a)   The fact that sales are less in quantity than expected will affect the department which store stock (there will be more!) and/or the production department (they may have to revise their plans and make less).

(b)   Although the quantity sold is below budget, the sales revenue is more than budget. Whether or not the sales manager receives his bonus will depend on how the company defines 'successful' for this purpose.

Answer 1.9

VARIANCE REPORT PRODUCTION COST CENTRES APRIL 20X1	
	Year to 30 April 20X1 £
Materials	4,038 (A)
Labour	4,022 (A)
Expenses	3,781 (A)
Comment The significant variances which are more than 10% from budget are: • Materials £4,038 (A) = 11.5% • Expenses £3,781 (A) = 25.2%	

Chapter 2

Answer 2.1

Tutorial note. In (a) the difference between the original net profit (£10,000) and the net loss of B is dropped (£40,000) is £50,000, the contribution of B.

B's contribution = Sales revenue – Variable costs
= £120,000 – £70,000
= £50,000

In (b) note that there are a number of different options. The point in (iv) about the allocation of fixed costs is something we can only mention briefly here, but you will study the issues in depth at Intermediate level.

(a)   If Product B is dropped, its variable costs (£70,000) will be saved but the fixed costs will still have to be paid.

	Product A £'000
Sales revenue	100
Less: Direct costs	(40)
Less: Fixed production overheads	(40)
Gross profit	20
Less: Other fixed costs	(60)
Net loss	(40)

(b)   The company could

(i)   Use the spare capacity freed by not producing Product B to make more of Product A
(ii)   Investigate the possibility of using the spare capacity to make a new product
(iii)   Raise the price of Product B
(iv)   Investigate the way fixed costs have been shared between the two products

Answer 2.2

Tutorial note. (d) introduces the idea that there is more to pricing decisions than purely mathematical calculations.

(a)   Each can contributes 10p (40p – 30p) to fixed costs.

(b)   It must sell 500,000 cans to cover fixed costs (£50,000 divided by 10p).

(c)   Budgeted profit will be £25,000 = (750,000 × 10p) – £50,000 (fixed costs).

(d)   If there is spare capacity in the factory then this order will contribute an extra £1,000 to profits (20,000 cans × contribution of 5p). It might, however, upset regular customers if they got to hear of it.

Answer 2.3

Tutorial note. Note the following features about the report.

(a) An introduction and terms of reference
(b) Stating of assumptions (using the office manager's forecasts)
(c) Report divided into clearly headed sections
(d) Clear conclusions with a recommended course of action

The report considers the purchase cost issue separately from maintenance. Note that the costs of one option (purchasing outright and not taking out a maintenance contract) are uncertain; risk is therefore involved in the decision.

Cash flow may also be important. Even if immediate purchase is significantly cheaper ultimately than the other options, it will still be too expensive if you cannot come up with the money now!

The report might look something like this.

FEASIBILITY REPORT FOR OFFICE DRINKS VENDING MACHINE

Terms of reference

1 To determine whether forecast sales will cover costs
2 To compare the benefits of purchase or leasing
3 To identify any other issues which need consideration

Introduction

1 This report was requested by the office manager
2 I have used her forecasts of selling prices and sales
3 Other information comes from the supplier's literature
4 My cost comparisons are made over 5 years

1 **Will forecast sales cover costs?**

Both coffee and tea are to be sold at 30p per cup. Coffee costs 22p per cup and tea 20p per cup. Forecast sales are 17,000 cups of coffee and 11,000 cups of tea per year.

	Coffee £	Tea £	Total £
Revenue	5,100	3,300	8,400
Less Variable costs	3,740	2,200	5,940
Contribution per year	1,360	1,100	2,460

A 5-year lease on the machine would cost £780 a year which would easily be covered. The total lease cost over 5 years would be £3,900.

Purchase of the machine would be £2,600 and would be covered in just over one year

2 **Maintenance**

Under the leasing contract, maintenance would be undertaken by the supplier so the total cost of £3,900 over five years is not affected by maintenance costs.

Outright purchase could be combined with a maintenance contract at £150 a year. This would bring the total cost over five years to £3,350.

Alternatively, we could call in a repairer as necessary but, since the cost is unknown, this would be a more risky option.

3   **Cash flow considerations**

Outright purchase of the machine, although cheaper in total, requires a larger outlay at the outset. The leasing contract would spread the outlay more evenly over the five years.

Conclusions

1   On forecast sales, the costs of the machine are easily covered whichever option is chosen.

2   Outright purchase without a maintenance contract is the cheapest but most risky option and puts the most pressure on immediate cash resources.

3   Adding the maintenance contract to purchase reduces the risk and is still cheaper than leasing.

4   The main benefit of leasing is to spread the cost evenly.

Recommendation

I recommend purchase of the machine and the annual maintenance contract.

Susan Scott

Answer 2.4

Tutorial note. Fixed costs need not be included in the calculations for pricing in this example. They remain the same whatever price is charged, that is they are not relevant to this decision. You will still get the same answer if you do include them, but it is quicker just to look at the contribution.

The price options will give the following results.

| | | | Contribution | |
| Sales volume | Price per unit | Variable cost per unit | Per unit | Total |
	£	£	£	£
29,000	4.00	2.20	1.80	52,200
25,000	4.50	2.20	2.30	57,500
20,000	5.00	2.20	2.80	56,000
17,000	5.50	2.20	3.30	56,100
15,000	6.00	2.20	3.80	57,000

A price of £4.50 will therefore give the highest profit.

If £6,000 is spent on advertising, then an extra 10% of sales can be achieved at this price.

This will only increase total contribution by 10% (£5,750) and is therefore not worth doing.

Chapter 3

Answer 3.1

Materials	Labour	Expenses
Saleable stocks	Petrol station staff	Heating
Carrier bags	Car park attendant	Lighting
Other packaging	Check-out staff	Telephone
Cleaning materials	Supervisors	Post
Bakery ingredients	Delicatessen staff	Stationery
	Bakery staff	Rent
	Shelf fillers	Business rates
	Warehouse staff	Water rates
	Cleaners	Vehicle running costs
	Security staff	Advertising
	Administrative staff	Discounts
	Managers	Bank charges
	Delivery staff	Waste disposal
	Maintenance staff	

Answer 3.2

(a)   Variable
(b)   Fixed
(c)   Fixed
(d)   Fixed
(e)   Variable

Answer 3.3

Tutorial note. Think about the type of production process involved and how costs would be collected.

- **A baker** would probably use batch costing. The cost units (loaves, cakes) are identical but would be produced in separately identifiable batches.

- **A transport company** would use unit costing, probably using a cost unit such as the tonne-kilometre (the cost of carrying one tonne for one kilometre).

- **A plumber** would use job costing, since every plumbing job is a separately identifiable cost unit.

- **An accountancy firm** would use job costing, since each client would require a different amount of time from employees of different skills.

- **A paint manufacturer** would use unit costing since the total costs incurred would be averaged over all the tins of paint produced in a period.

Answer 3.4

(a) A **cost unit** is a unit of product (or service) for which costs are ascertained.

(b) A **functional cost** is one that relates to a 'function' or area of operations of a business, for example production, administration, research, distribution and so on.

(c) A **fixed cost** is one that does not increase or decrease when a different number of units are produced.

(d) A **standard cost** is an estimate of what a cost should be on average in the future.

(e) An **indirect cost** is a cost that cannot be identified with one particular cost unit.

(f) An **overhead** is another name for an indirect cost (as explained in (e)).

(g) A **cost centre** is a location, a function (a person or a department), an activity or a piece of equipment which incurs costs that can be attributed to cost units.

(h) A **variable cost** is one that increases when more units are made and decreases when fewer units are made.

(i) A **direct cost** is one that can be traced directly to a cost centre or cost unit.

Chapter 4

Answer 4.1

(a) Metal, rubber, plastic, glass, fabric, oil, paint, glue

(b) Cereals, plastic, cardboard, glue. You might have included sugar and preservatives and so on, depending upon what you eat for breakfast

(c) Sand, gravel, cement, bricks, plaster, wood, metal, plastic, glass, slate

(d) You will have to mark your own answer. If you work for a service organisation like a firm of accountants, you could view the paper (and binding) of sets of accounts sent out to clients as raw materials, although in practice such materials are likely to be regarded as indirect costs

Answer 4.2

Direct materials can be traced directly to specific units of product or service whereas **indirect materials** cannot.

Answer 4.3

(a) Direct
(b) Direct
(c) Indirect
(d) Direct
(e) Direct

Answer 4.4

Raw materials are goods purchased for incorporation into products for sale, but not yet issued to production. **Work in progress** is the name given to the materials while they are in the course of being converted to the final product. **Finished goods** are the end products when they are ready to be sold.

Answer 4.5

Four from the following:

(a) The name and address of the ordering organisation
(b) The date of the order
(c) The order number
(d) The address and date for delivery or collection
(e) Details of the goods or services ordered

Answer 4.6

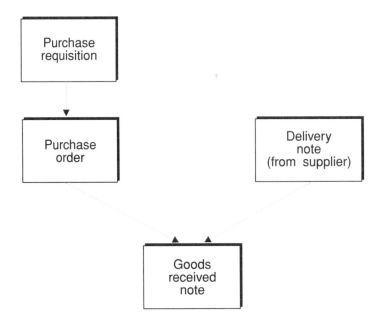

Answer 4.7

(a)   **FIFO**

Date of issue	Quantity Units	Value	£	Cost of issues £
4 May	200	100 at £2.00	200	
		100 at £2.10	210	
				410
11 May	400	300 at £2.10	630	
		100 at £2.12	212	
				842
20 May	100	100 at £2.12		212
Total cost of issues				1,464
Closing stock value	200	100 at £2.12	212	
		100 at £2.40	240	
				452
				1,916

The cost of materials issued plus the value of closing stock equals the cost of purchases plus the value of opening stock (£1,916).

(b)　**LIFO**

Date of issue	Quantity Units	Value	£	Cost of issues £
4 May	200	200 at £2.10		420
11 May	400	300 at £2.12	636	
		100 at £2.10	210	
				846
20 May	100	100 at £2.40		240
Total cost of issues				1,506
Closing stock value	200	100 at £2.10	210	
		100 at £2.00	200	
				410
				1,916

The cost of materials issued plus the value of closing stock equals the cost of purchases plus the value of opening stock (£1,916).

(c)　**Weighted average cost**

Date	Received Units	Issued Units	Balance Units	Total stock value £	Unit cost £	Price of issue £
Opening stock			100	200	2.00	
3 May	400			840	2.10	
			500*	1,040	2.08	
4 May		200		(416)	2.08	416
			300	624	2.08	
9 May	300			636	2.12	
			600*	1,260	2.10	
11 May		400		(840)	2.10	840
			200	420	2.10	
18 May	100			240	2.40	
			300*	660	2.20	
20 May		100		(220)	2.20	220
Cost of issues						1,476
Closing stock			200	440	2.20	440
						1,916

*　A new average unit cost is calculated whenever a new receipt of materials occurs.

The cost of materials issued plus the value of closing stock equals the cost of purchases plus the value of opening stock (£1,916).

Answer 4.8

(a)   **FIFO** has the disadvantage that if stocks are quite old they may be issued to production at a price which is well below the current market price. This gives the wrong message to production managers.

(b)   **LIFO** has the advantage that stock will be issued to production at a cost close to market value, thereby helping production managers gain a realistic idea of recent costs.

(c)   The **weighted average cost method** involves less cumbersome calculations than the other methods, but the issue price rarely represents an actual price that could be found in the market.

Answer 4.9

	Cost centre code no.	Expenditure code no.
Issue of packing materials to production	300	100
Issue of raw materials to machining centre	100	100
Issue of lubricating oils to maintenance	400	200
Issue of cleaning materials to finishing centre	200	200

Answer 4.10

Five from the following:

(a)   Stock quantities delivered may not have matched the quantity shown on the Goods Received Note, which is used to update the stock records.

(b)   The quantity of stock issued to production may not have matched the quantity on the materials requisition note.

(c)   Stock may have been returned to stores without documentation.

(d)   There may be other errors in the stock records (for example casting errors).

(e)   Stock may have been destroyed or broken without a record being made.

(f)   Stock may have been stolen.

Chapter 5

Answer 5.1

(a) From the information given, the only way of analysing Walter's time is as so many hours of 'general foreman duties'. In other words his work is so diverse that it is not possible to trace it as a direct cost to individual jobs.

It would be more appropriate to ensure that details of the individual jobs were recorded in such a way that Walter's time could be equitably split between them. For example a job requiring 20 men is likely to require twice as much of Walter's attention as a job requiring 10 men.

(b) Peter's time may at first seem to be as difficult to analyse as Walter's, but in fact it is probable that he could fill in a daily or weekly time sheet, splitting out his time between the various types of work that he does. For example he may spend 3 hours at the counter in the morning, and 1 hour filing and 2 hours dealing with correspondence in the afternoon.

Answer 5.2

Job 249

Employee	Hours	Rate £	Total £
George	14	8.20	114.80
Paul	49	7.40	362.60
			477.40

Job 250

Employee	Hours	Rate £	Total £
George	2	8.20	16.40
John	107	5.30	567.10
Ringo	74	6.50	481.00
			1,064.50

Answer 5.3

The direct labour cost is the gross basic wage, £1,327.42.

Answer 5.4

None of Dave's overtime premiums should be charged to overheads and therefore both Jenny and Mel are wrong in this instance. Since the customer specifically requested that overtime be worked on his job in order that it is completed as soon as possible, the overtime premium is a **direct cost** of the job.

Answer 5.5

OPERATION CARD

Operators Name Shah, L		Total Batch Quantity -
Clock No 7142		Start Time -
Pay week No 17	Date W/E XX/XX/XX	Stop Time -

Part No 713/V	Works Order No 14 AB
Opertion Drilling	Special Instructions -

Quantity Produced	No Rejected	Good Production	Rate	£
Monday 173	14	159	50p	79.50
Tuesday 131	2	129	40p	51.60
Wednesday 92	-	92	20p	18.40
Thursday 120	7	113	30p	33.90
Friday 145	5	140	40p	56.00

Insector ND	Operative LS
Foreman AN	Date XX/XX/XX

PRODUCTION CANNOT BE CLAIMED WITHOUT A PROPERLY SIGNED CARD

		£
Gross wage	=	79.50
		51.60
		18.40
		33.90
		56.00
		239.40

Answer 5.6

		£
Time rate = 35 hours × £8		280
Time allowed for 90 units (× 0.5 hour)	= 45 hours	
Therefore time saved	= 10 hours	
Bonus = 40% × 10 hours × £8		32
Total gross wages		312

PROFESSIONAL EDUCATION

Answer 5.7

Tutorial note. To decide on the correct code numbers, read the instructions carefully, and then make two decisions for each cost.

- Which cost centre should be charged with the labour cost?
- Is the labour cost a direct cost or an indirect cost?

WEEKLY TIME SHEET

Name *J. Wain*

Staff number: 1 7 2 5 4

Week ending: 0 9 1 2 0 1

	M	T	W	T	F	Hours	£	CODE
Direct time								
Finishing	5	4		1	3	13	143	1 0 1 0 0
Packing				6	3	9	99	2 0 1 0 0
Direct total	5	4		7	6	22	242	
Administration								
Budget meeting	2				1	3	33	
Total admin	2				1	3	33	3 0 2 0 0
Training and courses								
First Aid course		3				3	33	
Total training		3				3	33	4 0 2 0 0
Holidays, sickness								
Holiday			7			7	77	
Total leave			7			7	77	3 0 2 0 0
TOTAL	7	7	7	7	7	35	385	

Signed .... *RS* ....

Authorised .... *LW* ....

Chapter 6

Answer 6.1

(a)   Capital expenditure

(b)   Depreciation of a fixed asset is revenue expenditure.

(c)   The legal fees associated with the purchase of a property may be added to the purchase price and classified as capital expenditure. The cost of the premises in the balance sheet of the business will then include the legal fees.

(d)   Capital expenditure (enhancing an existing fixed asset)

(e)   Revenue expenditure

(f)   Capital expenditure

(g)   If customs duties are borne by the purchaser of the fixed asset, they may be added to the cost of the machinery and classified as capital expenditure.

(h)   Similarly, if carriage costs are paid for by the purchaser of the fixed asset, they may be included in the cost of the fixed asset and classified as capital expenditure.

(i)   Installation costs of a fixed asset are also added to the fixed asset's cost and classified as capital expenditure.

(j)   Revenue expenditure

Answer 6.2

You will need to ask the operational department concerned whether the machine is used **exclusively for one product** or for several different products.

If the machine is used exclusively for one product then the whole of the depreciation charge is traceable directly to that product and the depreciation is therefore a **direct expense**. If the machine is used for several different products and it is difficult to allocate the depreciation charges to each individual product then the depreciation charge should be an **indirect expense**.

Answer 6.3

Straight line method

$$\text{Depreciation per annum} = \frac{\text{Cost} - \text{residual value}}{\text{Expected life}}$$

$$= \frac{£(75,000 - 5,000)}{5 \text{ years}}$$

$$= £14,000$$

Reducing balance method

	£
Capital cost	75,000
Year 1 charge (£75,000 × 42%)	31,500
	43,500
Year 2 charge (£43,500 × 42%)	18,270
	25,230
Year 3 charge (£25,230 × 42%)	10,597
	14,633
Year 4 charge (£14,633 × 42%)	6,146
	8,487
Year 5 charge (£8,487 × 42%)	3,565
	4,922

Answer 6.4

	£	*Code*
Strange (Properties) Ltd	4,000.00	0120
Yorkshire Electricity plc	1,598.27	0060
Dudley Stationery Ltd	275.24	0100
Dora David (Cleaner)	125.00	0040
BPP Publishing Ltd	358.00	0030
AAT	1,580.00	0160
British Telecom	1,431.89	0170
Kall Kwik (Stationers)	312.50	0100
Interest to 31.3.X3	2,649.33	0020
L & W Office Equipment	24.66	0090
Avis	153.72	0190
Federal Express	32.00	0100
Starriers Garage Ltd	79.80	0070

Answer 6.5

The following expenses may be chargeable directly to clients.

	£	
Kall Kwik (Stationers)	312.50	Photocopying costs: say 200 sets of accounts to be sent to shareholders?
Avis	153.72	The cost of renting a car to travel on a client's business?

The following expenses *may* be chargeable directly to departments.

	£	
Dudley Stationery Ltd	275.24	If this type of stationery is used exclusively by one department.
L & W Office Equipment	24.66	If the item is used exclusively by one department.
Starriers Garage Ltd	79.80	The car is probably used by a specific employee.

Federal Express expenses could also fall into this category. The remaining items need to be split between departments. Training costs and AAT subscriptions could be split according to the specific staff involved, rent according to the floor area occupied and so on. (The next chapter goes into this in more detail.)

Chapter 7

Answer 7.1

(a)   **Absorption costing** is a method of determining a product cost that includes a proportion of all production overheads incurred in the making of the product and possibly a proportion of other overheads such as administration and selling overheads.

(b)   • **Allocation** of costs to cost centres
      • **Apportionment** of costs between cost centres
      • **Absorption** of costs into cost units

Answer 7.2

	Total	A	B	Assembly	Canteen	Mainten-ance	Basis of appor-tionment
	£	£	£	£	£	£	
Indirect wages	78,560	8,586	9,190	15,674	29,650	15,460	Actual
Consumable Materials	16,900	6,400	8,700	1,200	600	-	Actual
Rent and rates	16,700	3,711	4,453	5,567	2,227	742	Area
Insurance	2,400	533	640	800	320	107	Area
Power	8,600	4,730	3,440	258	-	172	Usage
Heat and light	3,400	756	907	1,133	453	151	Area
Depreciation	40,200	20,100	17,900	2,200	-	-	Value
	166,760	44,816	45,230	26,832	33,250	16,632	

Workings

(1)   **Rent and rates, insurance, heat and light**

Floor area is a sensible measure to use as the basis for apportionment.

	Area	Proportion total area	Share of rent & rates	Share of insurance	Share of heat & light
	Sq metres		£	£	£
Machine shop A	10,000	10/45	3,711	533	756
Machine shop B	12,000	12/45	4,453	640	907
Assembly	15,000	15/45	5,567	800	1,133
Canteen	6,000	6/45	2,227	320	453
Maintenance	2,000	2/45	742	107	151
	45,000		16,700	2,400	3,400

(2)   **Power**

	Percentage	Share of cost
	%	£
Machine shop A	55	4,730
Machine shop B	40	3,440
Assembly	3	258
Maintenance	2	172
		8,600

(3)   **Depreciation**

In the absence of specific information about the fixed assets in use in each department and the depreciation rates that are applied, this cost is shared out on the basis of the **relative value of each department's machinery** to the total. In practice more specific information would (or should) be available.

Answer 7.3

	Total	A	B	Assembly	Canteen	Mainten-ance	Basis of appor-tionment
	£	£	£	£	£	£	
Total overheads	166,760	44,816	45,230	26,832	33,250	16,632	
Reapportion (W1)	-	7,600	5,890	19,760	(33,250)	-	Dir labour
Reapportion (W2)	-	4,752	11,880	-	-	(16,632)	Mac usage
Totals	166,760	57,168	63,000	46,592	-	-	

Workings

(1)   **Canteen overheads**

Total direct labour hours = 35,000

$$\text{Machine shop A} = \frac{8,000}{35,000} \times £33,250 = £7,600$$

$$\text{Machine shop B} = \frac{6,200}{35,000} \times £33,250 = £5,890$$

$$\text{Assembly} = \frac{20,800}{35,000} \times £33,250 = £19,760$$

(2) **Maintenance overheads**

Total machine hours = 25,200

Machine shop A $= \dfrac{7,200}{25,200} \times £16,632 = £4,752$

Machine shop B $= \dfrac{18,000}{25,200} \times £16,632 = £11,880$

The total overhead has now been shared, on a fair basis, between the three production departments.

Answer 7.4

Direct apportionment method	Production 1	Production 2	Service 1	Service 2
	£	£	£	£
	97,428	84,947	9,384	15,823
Apportion Service 1 costs (20:15)	5,362	4,022	(9,384)	–
	102,790	88,969	-	15,823
Apportion Service 2 costs (3:8)	4,315	11,508	-	(15,823)
	107,105	100,477	-	-

Answer 7.5

Step-down method	Production 1	Production 2	Service 1	Service 2
	£	£	£	£
	97,428	84,947	9,384	15,823
Apportion Service 1 costs (20:15:5)	4,692	3,519	(9,384)	1,173
	102,120	88,466	-	16,996
Apportion Service 2 costs (3:8)	4,635	12,361	-	(16,996)
	106,755	100,827	-	-

Answer 7.6

(a) **Overhead absorption rate** $= \dfrac{\text{Expected overheads}}{\text{Planned direct labour hours}}$

$\dfrac{£108,000}{90,000} = £1.20$ per direct labour hour

(b) **Overhead absorption rate** $= \dfrac{\text{Expected overheads}}{\text{Planned direct machine hours}}$

$\dfrac{£720,000}{50,000} = £14.40$ per direct machine hour

Answer 7.7

		Domestic	Industrial
Direct labour cost per unit		£180	£80
Rate per hour		£10	£10
Direct labour hours per unit		18	8
Production volume (units)		20,000	20,000
Total labour hours		360,000	160,000

$$\text{Overhead absorption rate} = \frac{\text{Total overhead}}{\text{Total labour hours}} = \frac{£1,040,000}{(360,000 + 160,000)} = £2.00 \text{ per hour}$$

	Domestic	Industrial
	£	£
Direct materials	28	40
Direct labour	180	80
Direct expenses	40	200
Direct cost	248	320
Production overhead (18 × £2.00)/(8 × £2.00)	36	16
	284	336

Answer 7.8

		£	£
Actual expenditure			176,533
Overhead absorbed			
Machine shop A	7,300 hrs × £7.94	57,962	
Machine shop B	18,700 hrs × £3.50	65,450	
Assembly	21,900 hrs × £2.24	49,056	
			172,468
Under-absorbed overhead			4,065

Chapter 8

Activity 8.1

Entries in a wages control account would include total cost of payroll plus employer's national insurance contributions. Entries would also include transfers to work in progress accounts in respect of direct labour, and transfers to overhead accounts in respect of indirect labour.

Answer 8.2

(a) **Tutorial note**. Since we are given no information on the issue of direct materials we need to construct a stores ledger control account.

STORES LEDGER CONTROL ACCOUNT

	£		£
Balance b/f	18,500	Creditors/cash (returns)	2,300
Creditors/cash	142,000	Overhead accounts (indirect materials)	25,200
		WIP (balancing figure)	116,900
		Balance c/f	16,100
	160,500		160,500

The value of the issue of direct materials during April 20X0 was £116,900.

(b) The issue of direct materials would therefore be recorded as follows.

DR	WIP control account	£116,900
CR	Stores ledger control account	£116,900

Answer 8.3

Tutorial note. The depreciation provision is a production overhead cost incurred which is debited to the production overhead control account.

PRODUCTION OVERHEAD CONTROL ACCOUNT

	£		£
Bank account	125,478	Work in progress (27,000 × £5)	135,000
Depreciation	4,100		
Profit and loss account	5,422		
	135,000		135,000

The production overhead is over absorbed by £5,422. This amount is transferred, at the end of the period, as a credit in the profit and loss account.

Answer 8.4

(a)			£	£
	DEBIT	Materials stock	10,000	
	CREDIT	Creditors		10,000
(b)	DEBIT	Finished goods stock	50,000	
	CREDIT	Work in progress stock		50,000
(c)	DEBIT	Administration overhead/indirect materials	5,000	
	CREDIT	Materials stock		5,000
(d)	DEBIT	Production overhead control	20,000	
	CREDIT	Wages control		20,000

Answer 8.5

STORES LEDGER CONTROL ACCOUNT

	£		£
Opening balance b/f	24,175	Work in progress control	
Creditors control		(materials issued)	29,630
(materials purchased)	76,150	Closing stock c/f	70,695
	100,325		100,325

WORK IN PROGRESS CONTROL ACCOUNT

	£		£
Opening balance b/f	19,210	Finished goods control	
Stores ledger account		(cost of goods transferred)	62,130
(materials issued)	29,630	Closing stock c/f	24,800
Wages control			
(direct wages)	15,236		
Production overhead control			
(overhead absorbed			
15,236 × 150%)	22,854		
	86,930		86,930

FINISHED GOODS CONTROL ACCOUNT

	£		£
Opening balance b/f	34,164	Profit and loss account	
Work in progress control		(cost of sales)	59,830
(cost of goods completed)	62,130	Closing stock c/f	36,464
	96,294		96,294

PRODUCTION OVERHEAD CONTROL ACCOUNT

	£		£
Wages control (indirect workers wages)	9,462	Work in progress control (overheads absorbed)	22,854
Creditors control (other overheads incurred)	16,300	Profit and loss account (under-absorbed overhead) (bal.)	2,908
	25,762		25,762

CREDITORS CONTROL ACCOUNT

	£		£
Cash account (payments)	58,320	Opening balance b/f	15,187
Creditors c/f	49,317	Stores ledger control (materials purchased)	76,150
		Production overhead control (other overheads)	16,300
	107,637		107,637

PROFIT AND LOSS ACCOUNT

	£		£
Finished goods control (cost of goods sold)	59,830	Sales	75,400
Gross profit c/f	15,570		
	75,400		75,400
Selling and distribution overheads	5,240	Gross profit b/f	15,570
Production overhead control (under-absorbed overhead)	2,908		
Net profit c/f	7,422		
	15,570		15,570

Chapter 9

Answer 9.1

A job is a cost unit which consists of a single order (or contract) usually carried out in accordance with the special requirements of each customer. This means that each job will be at least slightly different from every other job and so separate records must be maintained to show the details of a particular job.

Tutorial note. You may have compiled a totally different list of examples of jobs.

Examples are numerous.

(a)   A haircut
(b)   The Channel Tunnel
(c)   A tailor-made suit
(d)   An audit
(e)   Jobs done by domestic plumbers, builders and so on

Answer 9.2

The documents most likely to be needed to establish *direct* costs are the materials requisition note, M Bobb's time sheet and the sub-contractor's invoice.

Details of materials used could probably, but not necessarily, have been obtained from the stock card too. The payroll would not be analysed in sufficient detail. The cost of electricity is not (so far as we are told) *directly* traceable to the job in question. The GRN and the clock card are of no relevance. The skip hire invoice appears to be an ongoing cost, not directly traceable to this job.

Answer 9.3

(a)

	£
Direct material Y (400 kilos × £5)	2,000
Direct material Z (800 − 60 kilos × £6)	4,440
Total direct material cost	6,440

(b)

	£
Department P (300 hours × £4)	1,200
Department Q (200 hours × £5)	1,000
Total direct labour cost	2,200

Overtime premium will be charged to overhead in the case of Department P, and to the job of the customer who asked for overtime to be worked in the case of Department Q.

(c)

	£
Direct material cost	6,440
Direct labour cost	2,200
Production overhead (500 hours × £3)	1,500
	10,140

Answer 9.4

Tutorial note. Note that the profit margin is given as a percentage on selling price. If profit is 25% on selling price, this is the same as 33 $\frac{1}{3}$% (25/75) on cost.

			Job TN8 £		Job KT2 £
Direct material			154.00		108.00
Direct labour:	dept X	(20 × 3.80)	76.00	(16 × 3.80)	60.80
	dept Y	(12 × 3.50)	42.00	(10 × 3.50)	35.00
	dept Z	(10 × 3.40)	34.00	(14 × 3.40)	47.60
Total direct cost			306.00		251.40
Overhead:	dept X	(20 × 12.86)	257.20	(16 × 12.86)	205.76
	dept Y	(12 × 12.40)	148.80	(10 × 12.40)	124.00
	dept Z	(10 × 14.03)	140.30	(14 × 14.03)	196.42
Total cost			852.30		777.58
Profit			284.10		259.19
Quoted selling price			1,136.40		1,036.77

Answer 9.5

(a) *Big units*

	£	£
Direct materials		5,240
Direct labour		
Skilled 1,580 hours at £5	7,900	
Semi-skilled 3,160 hours at £4	12,640	
		20,540
Direct expenses		1,180
Administrative expenses		
4,740 hours at £0.50 (see below)*		2,370
		29,330
Selling price		33,180
Calculated profit		3,850
Divided: Staff bonus 20%		770
Profit for company 80%		3,080

$$\text{*Administrative expenses absorption rate} \quad = \quad \frac{£4,400}{8,800} \text{ per labour hour}$$

$$= \quad £0.50 \text{ per labour hour}$$

(b)

		Little units			All-purpose	
		£	£		£	£
Direct materials			6,710			3,820
Direct labour						
Skilled	1,700 hrs at £5	8,500		160 hrs at £5	800	
Semi-skilled	1,900 hrs at £4	7,600		300 hrs at £4	1,200	
Direct expenses		1,700			250	
Administration						
expenses:	3,600 hrs at £0.50	1,800		460 hrs at £0.50	230	
		19,600			2,480	
Costs to						
Completion	20/80 × 19,600	4,900		75/25 × 2,480	7,440	
			24,500			9,920
Total costs			31,210			13,740
Selling price			27,500			19,500
Calculated						
profit/(loss)			(3,710)			5,760
Divided:	Staff bonus 20%		-			1,152
	(Loss)/profit for company		(3,710)			4,608

Note that whilst direct labour costs, direct expenses and administration expenses increase in proportion to the total labour hours required to complete the little units and the all-purpose units, there will be no further material costs to complete the batches.

(c)   Little units are projected to incur a loss. There are two possible reasons for the loss.

(i)   The estimation process may be inadequate. For example, it may have been incorrect to assume that the make-up of the costs to completion is the same as the make-up of the costs already incurred. It is possible that all of the skilled work has already been carried out and only unskilled labour is required to complete the batch.

(ii)   The loss is a result of inadequate estimating. If so, the estimation procedure should be reviewed to prevent recurrence.

(iii)   It is the result of a lack of cost control. If this is the case, appropriate action should be taken to exercise control in future.

Chapter 10

Answer 10.1

(a)   A standard cost is standard in two senses.

    (i)   It is a uniform cost that is applied to all like items, irrespective of their actual cost.
    (ii)   It is a measure of expected performance, that is, a standard to be achieved.

(b)   Standard costing is used for two main reasons.

    (i)   As a means of valuing stocks and the cost of production.
    (ii)   In variance analysis, which is a means of controlling the business.

Answer 10.2

Tutorial note. This activity is a test of your ability to analyse information in a way that avoids laborious computations as much as a test of your understanding of standard setting. The operation is done by grade X labour at £4.80 per hour unless otherwise indicated.

Operation	Grade	Rate £	Time Hours	Cost £
1			1.50	7.20
2	Y	5.50	1.00	5.50
3			0.25	1.20
4	Z	6.50	2.00	13.00
5			0.50	2.40
6	Y	5.50	2.00	11.00
7	Z	6.50	3.00	19.50
8			1.00	4.80
9			0.25	1.20
10	Y	5.50	0.50	2.75

	A £	B £	C £	Sharp C £	D £	E £	F £	Augmented F £	G £
1				7.20	7.20			7.20	7.20
2	5.50	5.50			5.50				
3			1.20	1.20		1.20		1.20	
4	13.00			13.00		13.00	13.00		
5	2.40	2.40				2.40			2.40
6		11.00	11.00	11.00	11.00			11.00	
7					19.50			19.50	
8			4.80					4.80	
9			1.20				1.20		1.20
10		2.75			2.75	2.75			2.75
Standard cost	20.90	21.65	18.20	32.40	45.95	19.35	21.40	36.50	13.55

Answer 10.3

Tutorial note. Read the data carefully. The standard times are provided in terms of **minutes**. You need to convert your final answer to **hours**.

Standard hours produced		Standard hours
Burger meals: $\dfrac{2,400 \times 10 \text{ minutes}}{60}$ =		400
Chicken meals: $\dfrac{1,300 \times 15 \text{ minutes}}{60}$ =		325
Total standard hours produced		725

Answer 10.4

STANDARD COST CARD - PRODUCT TUDOR

Direct materials	*Cost*	*Requirement*	£	£
A	£1 per kg	7 kgs	7	
B	£2 per litre	4 litres	8	
C	£3 per m	3 m	9	
				24
Direct labour				
Skilled	£10 per hour	8 hours	80	
Semi-skilled	£5 per hour	4 hours	20	
				100
Standard direct cost				124
Variable production overhead	£2.50 per hour	8 hours		20
Standard variable cost of production				144
Fixed production overhead	£6.25 (W) per hour	8 hours		50
Standard full production cost				194

Working

Overhead absorption rate = $\dfrac{£250,000}{5,000 \times 8}$ = £6.25 per skilled labour hour

Answer 10.5

Standard product cost and gross profit

	£
Direct material L	300
Direct material W	270
Direct labour	165
Direct cost	735
Production overhead (£252,000/1,200)	210
Total product cost	945
Selling price (£120,000/(1,200/12))	1,200
Gross profit	255

Answer 10.6

(a)   The *ideal standard*, based on the most favourable operating conditions, seems to be one hour. This is the time achieved by Jed less the 15 minutes idle time (since we are not sure it is *completely* unavoidable). However, in view of the other performances it seems unlikely that anybody could achieve this. Further investigation should be made to determine whether Jed's two attempts include idle time or not: it may be that they were rare occasions when idle time was avoided.

(b)   The *current standard* can be taken as the average (the arithmetic mean) of all the times recorded.

Worker	Time Minutes	Time Minutes
Lynn	105	120
Alison	125	115
Jed	75	75
Kate	130	90
Nick	105	97
Edmund	99	117
Bob	120	90
Roger	135	103
Tina	80	95
Tim	140	122
Clive	95	112
Graham	119	125
Barry	100	120
Glen	117	113
	1,545	1,494

Arithmetic mean $= \dfrac{(1,545 + 1,494)}{2 \times 14} = 108.5$ minutes $= 1$ hour 48 minutes

(c)   An *attainable standard* is one that makes some allowance for wastage and inefficiencies. Simply by looking at the times we can see that most come roughly in the range 1 hour 40 minutes to 2 hours. (1 hour 35 minutes to 2 hours if you do know how to calculate quartiles). A reasonably attainable standard would therefore be 1 hour 40 minutes or slightly less, giving most staff something to aim for.

(d) The *basic standard* is given in the question as 2 hours and 30 minutes. This is clearly very outdated and of little value.

Answer 10.7

(a)

Material	Standard cost £	Guildford £	Dorking £	Reigate £	Coulsdon £
AB30	1.68	33.60	33.60	16.80	8.40
AB35	5.93	-	59.30	-	-
BB29	15.00	-	-	60.00	-
BB42	2.40	19.20	12.00	-	28.80
CA19	20.07	401.40	180.63	-	100.35
CD26	2.50	15.00	-	7.50	-
Total standard materials cost		469.20	285.53	84.30	137.55

(b)

Material	Supplier	Information source	Unit cost £	20X2 standard £	20X3 standard £	Note
AB30	4073	20X3 catalogue	1.74	1.68	1.74	(i)
AB35	4524	20X2 catalogue	5.93	5.93		
		Invoice (10/X2)	6.05		6.27	(ii)
		Telephone enquiry to 4524	6.00			
BB29	4333	X2/X3 catalogue	15.72	15.00	16.30	(iii)
BB42	4929	Invoice (5/X2)	2.36	2.40		
	-	New supplier quotation (11/X2)	1.94		2.01	(iv)
CA19	4124	Contract to 12/X3	20.07	20.07	20.07	(v)
		Invoice (12/X2)	21.50			
CD26	4828	-		2.50	2.59	(vi)

Notes

(i) AB30 is costed on the basis of the 20X3 catalogue price which is assumed to be guaranteed for 12 months.

(ii) AB35's new standard cost is on the basis of the most recent invoiced cost plus 3.7%. (The telephone enquiry figure is suspiciously 'round'.)

(iii) BB29's current standard cost looks like an underestimate. Do not allow this to influence your calculation for 20X3.

(iv) BB42 should be bought from the new supplier, on the evidence available. The standard cost is £1.94 plus 3.7%.

(v) For CA19 the contractually agreed price should be used as the standard cost. Enquiries should be made as to why this was not the cost invoiced in December 20X2.

(vi) In the absence of other information 3.7% is added to the 20X2 standard cost for CD26.

Chapter 11

Answer 11.1

Tutorial note. Don't forget to indicate whether your calculated variance is adverse or favourable.

	£
100 units should cost (× £10)	1,000
but did cost	1,025
Material total variance	25 (A)

	£
520 kg should cost (× £2)	1,040
but did cost	1,025
Material price variance	15 (F)

100 units should use (× 5kg)	500 kgs
but did use	520 kgs
Material usage variance (in kgs)	20 kgs (A)
× standard price (per kg)	× £2
Materials usage variance (in £)	£40 (A)

Answer 11.2

	£
106,000 kgs should cost (× £5)	530,000
but did cost	530,500
Materials price variance	500 (A)
10,000 units should have used (× 10 kgs)	100,000 kgs
but did use	106,000 kgs
Material usage variance (in kilos)	6,000 kgs (A)
× standard price per kilo	× £5
Material usage variance (in £)	£30,000 (A)

	£
50,200 hours should have cost (× £6)	301,200
but did cost	307,200
Labour rate variance	6,000 (A)
10,000 units should take (× 5 hours)	50,000 hrs
but did take	50,200 hrs
Labour efficiency variance (in hours)	200 hrs (A)
× standard rate per hour	× £6
Labour efficiency variance (in £)	£1,200 (A)

Answer 11.3

The overhead absorption rate is $\dfrac{£70,000}{14,000}$ = £5 per unit, or £2.50 per hour

	£
Total fixed overhead incurred	67,500
Total fixed overhead absorbed (12,000 units × £5)	60,000
Under-absorbed overhead = total variance	7,500 (A)

	£
Budgeted fixed overhead expenditure	70,000
Actual fixed overhead expenditure	67,500
Expenditure variance	2,500 (F)
12,000 units should have taken (× 2 hrs)	24,000 hrs
But did take	28,400 hrs
Efficiency variance (in hrs)	4,400 hrs (A)
× standard absorption rate per hour	× £2.50
Efficiency variance (in £)	£11,000 (A)
Budgeted activity level	28,000 hrs
Actual activity level	28,400 hrs
Capacity variance (in hrs)	400 hrs (F)
× standard absorption rate per hour	× £2.50
Capacity variance (in £)	£1,000 (F)

Summary

	£
Expenditure variance	2,500 (F)
Efficiency variance	11,000 (A)
Capacity variance	1,000 (F)
Total variance	7,500 (A)

Answer 11.4

Tutorial note. The first step is to calculate the budgeted overhead absorption rate per standard hour produced. To do this you need to convert the budgeted production output into standard hours.

Budgeted standard hours of production:

	Std hours
Product S (4,200 × 10 minutes/60)	700
Product H (2,400 × 20 minutes/60)	800
	1,500

Budgeted overhead absorption rate = $\dfrac{£4,500}{1,500}$ = £3 per standard hour

(a)

	£
Budgeted overhead expenditure	4,500
Actual overhead expenditure	5,200
Overhead expenditure variance	700 (A)

(b)   Actual production volume achieved: Std hours

Product S (3,600 × 10 minutes/60)	600
Product H (3,000 × 20 minutes/60)	1,000
	1,600

Overhead volume variance:

Actual production volume achieved	1,600 std hrs
Budgeted production volume	1,500 std hrs
Volume variance in std hrs	100 std hrs (F)
× absorption rate per std hour	× £3
Overhead volume variance	£300 (F)

(c)

Budgeted hours of work	1,500 hours
Actual hours worked	1,800 hours
Capacity variance in hours	300 hours (F)
× absorption rate per hour	× £3
Overhead capacity variance	£900 (F)

(d)

Standard time for output achieved	1,600 hours
Actual time taken	1,800 hours
Efficiency variance in hours	200 hours (A)
× absorption rate per hour	× £3
Overhead efficiency variance	£600 (A)

Check: Efficiency variance £600 (A) + Capacity variance £900 (F) = Volume variance £300(F).

Answer 11.5

(a) *Price variance - A*

	£
7,800 kgs should have cost (× £20)	156,000
but did cost	159,900
Price variance	3,900 (A)

Usage variance - A

800 units should have used (× 10 kgs)	8,000 kgs
but did use	7,800 kgs
Usage variance in kgs	200 kgs (F)
× standard price per kilogram	× £20
Usage variance in £	£4,000 (F)

Price variance - B

	£
4,300 litres should have cost (× £6)	25,800
but did cost	23,650
Price variance	2,150 (F)

Usage variance - B

800 units should have used (× 5 l)	4,000 Litres
but did use	4,300 Litres
Usage variance in litres	300 (A)
× standard price per litre	× £6
Usage variance in £	£1,800 (A)

(b) *Labour rate variance*

	£
4,200 hours should have cost (× £6)	25,200
but did cost	24,150
Rate variance	1,050 (F)

Labour efficiency variance

800 units should have taken (× 5 hrs)	4,000 hrs
but did take	4,200 hrs
Efficiency variance in hours	200 hrs (A)
× standard rate per hour	× £6
Efficiency variance in £	£1,200 (A)

(c) Overhead absorption rate per labour hour = £50/5 = £10
Budgeted overhead expenditure = £50 × 900 = £45,000
Actual output in standard hours = 800 × 5 = 4,000 standard hours

Fixed overhead expenditure variance

	£
Budgeted fixed overhead expenditure	45,000
Actual fixed overhead expenditure	47,000
Fixed overhead expenditure variance	2,000 (A)

Fixed overhead volume variance

Actual production volume achieved	800 units
Budgeted production volume	900 units
Volume variance in units	100 units (A)
× standard absorption rate per unit	× £50
Fixed overhead volume variance	£5,000 (A)

Fixed overhead efficiency variance

From labour efficiency variance:	200 hours (A)
Efficiency variance in hours	× £10
× standard absorption rate per hour	
Fixed overhead efficiency variance	£2,000 (A)

Fixed overhead capacity variance

Budgeted hours of work (900 units × 5 hrs)	4,500 hrs
Actual hours worked	4,200 hrs
Capacity variance in hours	300 hrs (A)
× standard absorption rate per hour	× £10
Fixed overhead capacity variance	£3,000 (A)

Answer 11.6

(a) Two possible reasons are a price increase and careless purchasing (failing to take a discount, using the wrong supplier and so on). A third is that a higher quality of material was purchased deliberately.

(b) The temporary labour is likely to be paid a lower rate than standard, leading to a favourable labour rate variance. However, the temporary staff are likely to be less efficient than experienced staff, resulting in an adverse labour efficiency variance and perhaps an adverse material usage variance also.

See overleaf for information on other
BPP products and how to order

AAT Order

To BPP Professional Education, Aldine Place, London W12 8AW
Tel: 020 8740 2211. Fax: 020 8740 1184
E-mail: Publishing@bpp.com Web:www.bpp.com

Mr/Mrs/Ms (Full name)
Daytime delivery address
Postcode
E-mail
Daytime Tel

	5/04 Texts	5/04 Kits	Special offer	8/04 Passcards	Success CDs
FOUNDATION (£14.95 except as indicated)				Foundation	
Units 1 & 2 Receipts and Payments	☐	☐		£6.95 ☐	£14.95 ☐
Unit 3 Ledger Balances and Initial Trial Balance	☐ (Combined Text & Kit)		Foundation Sage Bookeeping and Excel Spreadsheets CD-ROM free if ordering all Foundation Text and Kits, including, Units 21 and 22/23 ☐		
Unit 4 Supplying Information for Mgmt Control	☐ (Combined Text & Kit)				
Unit 21 Working with Computers (£9.95)	☐				
Unit 22/23 Healthy Workplace/Personal Effectiveness (£9.95)	☐				
Sage and Excel for Foundation (Workbook with CD-ROM £9.95)	☐				
INTERMEDIATE (£9.95 except as indicated)					
Unit 5 Financial Records and Accounts	☐	☐		£5.95 ☐	£14.95 ☐
Unit 6/7 Costs and Reports (Combined Text £14.95)	☐	☐		£5.95 ☐	
Unit 6 Costs and Revenues	☐				£14.95 ☐
Unit 7 Reports and Returns	☐				
TECHNICIAN (£9.95 except as indicated)					
Unit 8/9 Core Managing Performance and Controlling Resources	☐			£5.95 ☐	£14.95 ☐
Spreadsheets for Technician (Workbook with CD-ROM)	☐ (Combined Text & Kit)		Spreadsheets for Technicians CD-ROM free if take Unit 8/9 Text and Kit ☐		
Unit 10 Core Managing Systems and People (£14.95)	☐	☐		£5.95 ☐	£14.95 ☐
Unit 11 Option Financial Statements (A/c Practice)	☐	☐		£5.95 ☐	
Unit 12 Option Financial Statements (Central Govnmt)	☐	☐		£5.95 ☐	
Unit 15 Option Cash Management and Credit Control	☐	☐		£5.95 ☐	
Unit 17 Option Implementing Audit Procedures	☐			£5.95 ☐	
Unit 18 Option Business Tax FA04 (8/04) (£14.95)	☐ (Combined Text & Kit)				
Unit 19 Option Personal Tax FA04 (8/04) (£14.95)	☐ (Combined Text & Kit)				
TECHNICIAN 2003 (£9.95)					
Unit 18 Option Business Tax FA03 (8/03 Text & Kit)	☐	☐			
Unit 19 Option Personal Tax FA03 (8/03 Text & Kit)	☐	☐			
SUBTOTAL	£	£	£	£	£

TOTAL FOR PRODUCTS £ ☐

POSTAGE & PACKING

Texts/Kits	First	Each extra
UK	£3.00	£3.00
Europe*	£6.00	£4.00 £
Rest of world	£20.00	£10.00 £
Passcards		
UK	£2.00	£1.00 £
Europe*	£3.00	£2.00 £
Rest of world	£8.00	£8.00 £
Success CDs		
UK	£2.00	£1.00 £
Europe*	£3.00	£2.00 £
Rest of world	£8.00	£8.00 £

TOTAL FOR POSTAGE & PACKING £ ☐
(Max £12 Texts/Kits/Passcards - deliveries in UK)

Grand Total (Cheques to *BPP Professional Education*)
I enclose a cheque for (incl. Postage) £ ☐
Or charge to Access/Visa/Switch
Card Number ☐☐☐☐ CV2 No ☐☐☐ last 3 digits on signature strip
Expiry date ☐☐☐☐ Start Date ☐☐☐☐
Issue Number (Switch Only) ☐☐
Signature

We aim to deliver to all UK addresses inside 5 working days; a signature will be required. Orders to all EU addresses should be delivered within 6 working days. All other orders to overseas addresses should be delivered within 8 working days. * Europe includes the Republic of Ireland and the Channel Islands.

See overleaf for information on other
BPP products and how to order

AAT Order

To BPP Professional Education, Aldine Place, London W12 8AW
Tel: 020 8740 2211. Fax: 020 8740 1184
E-mail: Publishing@bpp.com Web:www.bpp.com

Mr/Mrs/Ms (Full name) _____
Daytime delivery address _____
Postcode _____
Daytime Tel _____   E-mail _____

OTHER MATERIAL FOR AAT STUDENTS

	8/04 Texts	3/03 Text	3/04 Text

FOUNDATION (£5.95)

Basic Maths and English ☐

INTERMEDIATE (£5.95)

Basic Bookkeeping (for students exempt from Foundation) ☐

FOR ALL STUDENTS (£5.95)

Building Your Portfolio (old standards)	☐	
Building Your Portfolio (new standards)		☐
Basic Costing		☐

AAT PAYROLL

Finance Act 2004 8/04		Finance Act 2003 9/03
December 2004 and June 2005 assessments		June 2004 exams only

Special offer
Take Text and Kit together £44.95 ☐   (FA 2004)
Special offer
Take Text and Kit together £44.95 ☐   (FA 2003)

For assessments in 2005 £44.95 ☐
For assessments in 2004 £44.95 ☐

LEVEL 2 Text (£29.95)	☐
LEVEL 2 Kit (£19.95)	☐
LEVEL 3 Text (£29.95)	☐
LEVEL 3 Kit (£19.95)	☐

SUBTOTAL   £ _____   £ _____   £ _____

TOTAL FOR PRODUCTS   £ _____

POSTAGE & PACKING

Texts/Kits	First	Each extra
UK	£3.00	£3.00
Europe*	£6.00	£4.00
Rest of world	£20.00	£10.00
Passcards		
UK	£2.00	£1.00
Europe*	£3.00	£2.00
Rest of world	£8.00	£8.00
Tapes		
UK	£2.00	£1.00
Europe*	£3.00	£2.00
Rest of world	£8.00	£8.00

TOTAL FOR POSTAGE & PACKING   £ _____
(Max £12 Texts/Kits/Passcards - deliveries in UK)

Grand Total (Cheques to *BPP Professional Education*)   £ _____

I enclose a cheque for (incl. Postage)
Or charge to Access/Visa/Switch
Card Number ☐☐☐☐ ☐☐☐☐ ☐☐☐☐ ☐☐☐☐   CV2 No ☐☐☐ last 3 digits on signature strip

Expiry date _____   Start Date _____

Issue Number (Switch Only) _____

Signature _____

We aim to deliver to all UK addresses inside 5 working days; a signature will be required. Orders to all EU addresses should be delivered within 6 working days. All other orders to overseas addresses should be delivered within 8 working days. * Europe includes the Republic of Ireland and the Channel Islands.

Review Form & Free Prize Draw – AAT Basic Costing (4/04)

All original review forms from the entire BPP range, completed with genuine comments, will be entered into one of two draws on 31 January 2005 and 31 July 2005. The names on the first four forms picked out on each occasion will be sent a cheque for £50.

Name: _____   Address: _____

_____

_____

How have you used this Interactive Text?
(Tick one box only)

☐ Home study (book only)

☐ On a course: college _____

☐ With 'correspondence' package

☐ Other _____

Why did you decide to purchase this Interactive Text? *(Tick one box only)*

☐ Have used BPP Texts in the past

☐ Recommendation by friend/colleague

☐ Recommendation by a lecturer at college

☐ Saw advertising

☐ Other _____

During the past six months do you recall seeing/receiving any of the following?
(Tick as many boxes as are relevant)

☐ Our advertisement in *Accounting Technician* magazine

☐ Our advertisement in *Pass*

☐ Our brochure with a letter through the post

Which (if any) aspects of our advertising do you find useful?
(Tick as many boxes as are relevant)

☐ Prices and publication dates of new editions

☐ Information on Interactive Text content

☐ Facility to order books off-the-page

☐ None of the above

Your ratings, comments and suggestions would be appreciated on the following areas

	Very useful	Useful	Not useful
Introduction	☐	☐	☐
Chapter contents lists	☐	☐	☐
Examples	☐	☐	☐
Activities and answers	☐	☐	☐
Key learning points	☐	☐	☐
Quick quizzes and answers	☐	☐	☐

	Excellent	Good	Adequate	Poor
Overall opinion of this Text	☐	☐	☐	☐

Do you intend to continue using BPP Interactive Texts/Assessment Kits?   ☐ Yes   ☐ No

Please note any further comments and suggestions/errors on the reverse of this page.

The BPP author of this edition can be e-mailed at: janiceross@bpp.com

Please return this form to: Janice Ross, BPP Professional Education, FREEPOST, London, W12 8BR

Review Form & Free Prize Draw (continued)

Please note any further comments and suggestions/errors below

Free Prize Draw Rules

1   Closing date for 31 January 2005 draw is 31 December 2004. Closing date for 31 July 2005 draw is 30 June 2005.

2   Restricted to entries with UK and Eire addresses only. BPP employees, their families and business associates are excluded.

3   No purchase necessary. Entry forms are available upon request from BPP Professional Education. No more than one entry per title, per person. Draw restricted to persons aged 16 and over.

4   Winners will be notified by post and receive their cheques not later than 6 weeks after the relevant draw date.

5   The decision of the promoter in all matters is final and binding. No correspondence will be entered into.